MW01641107

Creative Collaborations

How to Form Lasting and Lucrative Partnerships without Being Smarmy

Kirsten Oliphant

Cover by James at http://goonwrite.com

To Rob.

Just as Data's dad in *The Goonies* said that Data was his best invention, YOU are MY best collaboration.

TABLE OF CONTENTS

Introduction

What Roller Derby Taught Me about Collaboration

I learned the secret to successful collaborations while playing roller derby.

I did not realize that I was learning this at the time. I was too busy trying to juke my way through the pack as a jammer or knock the other team's skaters to the ground.

But on the track, you aren't playing solo. Even as a jammer trying to break through walls. Or as a blocker trying to keep your point.

Roller derby is a team sport. It is THE most intense and intensive "hobby" that you could sign up for, taking up as many hours per week as a part-time job.

You wear the same color as your team. You practice the same hours. You carpool to practice. You give up family time, Netflix time, so.much.time.

You have team dinners and strategy sessions and play pranks on other teams. You have secret Facebook groups to talk smack. Your periods sync up. (*Yes, that is a thing.*)

And on the track, you see the evidence of all these off-track moments. You aren't four blockers. You are a WALL. Your jersey is soaked with sweat, but it's not just yours. You are that close with the other skaters.

You'll find fingerprint bruises on your arm the next day from your teammates, holding you close, pushing you in for a block, using you for a whip to cut through the pack.

You touch a lot of people's butts in roller derby. And this is not weird. A pat on the butt after a jam is great encouragement. You might rest your hand there in a wall, ready to push yourself or another blocker into the right position.

This is a metaphor, of course, so let me bring it back around to collaboration.

Touching other people's butts becomes commonplace in roller derby. Pushing and pulling teammates into place. Patting someone to say good game or better luck next jam.

You might pat your teammate on the butt at the bar when you are not in uniform, just because you don't even think about it anymore. It is simply how you say hello. You might pat your husband on the butt in church when you stand for a hymn and realize half a second later that you have become a little too accustomed to butt touching.

The taboo is lifted. The hesitation is gone. The sense of personal space and the wall that exists between people evaporates. Being part of a team takes away the strict sense of what is yours alone. You are together. You are one. And great teams embody this sense of oneness and unity.

All of which is to say that the secret to successful collaborations is TRUST.

This is what I learned from so many years on the track as a player and on the bench as a coach. Your team is only ever as good as the trust you have for one another. Rogue players, even great players, playing singularly hurt the team as a whole. They don't just break apart strong defensive walls; they break trust.

For the past five years I have learned something of trust in the online space. With writers and bloggers and podcasters. Men and women of different ages and different political views and in different niches.

I've been burned and had my work stolen. I've had people promise things and then lie when that promise is no longer convenient. I've seen my own jealousy creep up and wreck things—mostly wreck myself. I've seen partnerships fizzle and fail and I've felt the distinct loss of friendships.

But I've seen beautiful things too. I've been pushed farther and pushed faster through strategic partnerships and friendships. I've been inspired by the community, especially here in Houston through Houston Bloggers and Houston Social Media Breakfast. I have been the recipient of encouragement, praise I didn't deserve, and propelled forward into spaces that I could not have reached on my own.

The thing about trust is that it's risky. And if you've been burned by a partnership that turned sour, you may be even more hesitant to take the risk. Maybe you've never seen the amazing benefits that can come from great collaborations.

I hope this book will give you a few things: encouragement to actually do the sometimes hard and risky work of collaboration, inspiration for the kinds of partnerships you might have, and the tools to get started.

As a wise man once said: Stop. Collaborate. (And listen.)

Here's to your future partnerships and successful collaborations!

Because not everything can fit inside the pages of a book, you can find bonus resources and more here: http://createifwriting.com/collabbonus

1

You're Going the Wrong Way

One of my favorite movies as a kid was "Planes, Trains, and Automobiles." In one scene John Candy has somehow managed to get his car on the wrong side of a deserted highway at night. He is literally going in the wrong direction.

People in a car on the other side of the median pull up alongside and shout, "You're going the wrong way!"

He and Steve Martin brush off their concerns. "Oh, he's drunk," John Candy's character says. "How would he know where we're going?"

Only when Steve Martin's character sees the snowy median stretching between the two cars does he realize that they are literally driving in the wrong direction.

(Just for fun, you can watch this clip in the bonus section – http://createifwriting.com/collabbonus)

When it comes to collaborations, I see a lot of people going the wrong way. But until you see the headlights of an approaching vehicle (*metaphorically speaking*) or someone shouts at you, it's possible to just keep driving in the wrong way.

Working with other people is not a new or novel idea. In the online space everything is about connections: connecting with readers, connecting with other people doing what we are doing, connecting with bigger brands or influencers. Connect, connect, connect. You can find a ton of blog posts and articles and likely even courses about how you can and should connect.

But often the tips are very general or, at worst, the advice is really terrible. I read people saying things like:

- Ask that blogger if they will add your awesome infographic in their post!
- Submit a guest post to a big blog!
- Approach a successful writer to see if she can take time to answer your questions (*for free*) over coffee!
- Email everyone who is ranking well for a search term and ask them to link to your blog post instead of one of their other links!

Every one of those examples is one I have either heard someone suggest or have seen hit my inbox multiple times. I always want to tell these people: You're going the wrong way!

Sometimes I do. I'll hit reply and ask if this strategy is really working for them. If I'm in a good mood, I'll offer some suggestions. If I'm feeling snarky I try not to reply because I will be less kind. Now I can refer them to this book.

So what is the right way? Let's have some fun first and talk about the wrong way.

An important note about this section:

If you have ever done any of these things, this is not meant to shame you!

I am the person who always wants someone to tell me about the spinach in my teeth. And then I'm instantly horrified and overly humiliated. So when I use humor here or exaggerate about these mistakes, it's to keep things light and not to make you feel terrible. You are amazing!

If you continue to do these things, we can still be friends!

My way is not the only way. You may love a particular strategy that I say is a bad idea. Ultimately, we all need to do what works for US. But I do hope this section at least makes you think about what you're doing and how effective it is in the long run.

Some of these things may be effective, to a point.

The reason that so many people are emailing me about their infographics is because this must work for them some of the time. I am more interested in establishing long-term, beneficial relationships, not temporary tactics.

SIGNS YOU MIGHT BE GOING THE WRONG WAY

Want to see some specific bad examples? Who doesn't! That's why people love the Fashion Police, right? I've got some specific examples (*without using names or urls*) that you can check out. Consider this my What Not to Wear—Digital Marketing edition.

I'm sharing a lot of personal examples because they make it more interesting. I promise, though, this isn't just a list of things that annoy me. (*Even though they also do annoy me.*) These are general practices that will often burn bridges before you even start building them.

You're using some version of the skyscraper method.

As far as I can tell, this method came from Brian Dean of Backlinko. Essentially, you research what posts are showing up in search for a particular topic that you are also writing about on your site. Then you email the writers of those other articles, asking them to add a link to your post in their post. *(You can read all about this here: https://backlinko.com/skyscraper-technique)*

The reason I don't like this method is that I get multiple emails DAILY from different people using this exact template to reach out to me. Literally, they will use the same exact words. They have copied and pasted the example from the link above or maybe from another training they have received.

This method MAY work for some and some people that I respect (*Brian Dean is a smart guy!*) use this. Darren Rowse of Problogger even recommended it on his podcast, so who am I to argue?

The difference is this: if Darren Rowse of Problogger emails me to ask me to add in his link, I will. Because it's Darren Rowse asking! If Random Blogger #2 I don't know sends me the exact same email I got from Random Blogger #1 an hour earlier, I'm not interested. I don't have time to check out websites for the quality of content. Often these emails come from people running low-quality sites (*at least in my experience*). So unless I already know your name (*in which case, do you NEED to still be doing this??*), I'm not going to add your link.

You're pitching guest posts to bloggers you don't know.

I don't have a lot of guest posts on either of my sites. But you'd never know that, since I get multiple emails every day proposing guest posts.

Blogs that have a lot of guest posts typically have a page or an informational area about the requirements or how to reach out. If a blog does not have this page and you don't know the blog author, sending this kind of cold pitch is a signal to that person that you haven't done your research (*more in a sec*), you aren't really interested in connecting, and you just want to use their platform. Not good for long-term relationships.

You're doing cold pitches, period.

Only on the rarest of occasions will I say yes to a cold pitch. Why? It's not because I'm the biggest person ever and don't have time for the little people. It's because I have five kids, am running two sites, hosting a podcast, writing books, creating courses, and trying to live a semi-normal life.

So unless the cold pitch is extraordinarily unique (*either in terms of the idea or the way it's presented or BOTH*), I likely don't have time to consider it. If there is an immediate or direct benefit, maybe. But often the cold pitches that come through the door are simply asking for things that would benefit the person asking.

You are reaching out without doing your homework.

This typically goes along with the cold pitches. When someone emails me to say that they read my post with moving tips and know my readers would LOVE their infographic/guest post/link about moving, I know they haven't looked at anything else on my site. Because I have literally ONE post about moving.

If you are going to propose any kind of collaboration, you have to do your homework. You should know more about the person than one blog post or even one social media platform. You should check out their About page or even the Contact page to see what pertinent information they might share. They might have specifics about how to reach out. Or they might have just posted on Twitter that their mom died.

Do your research. It's simple, but it is significant.

You're asking someone to do something that really only benefits YOU.

Virtual summits have been going crazy the past few years *(and in part 2 of this book you'll get some tips if you want to run one!)*. There are some great summits and then there are some "other" summits. All summits have benefits to the host, the speakers, and the audience. But the "other" summits are clearly put on to benefit the host above all else.

Someone asked me to speak at her "other" summit with a list of requirements: how often I had to post, what my list size needed to be, etc. I had never heard of this person and her own online presence seemed fairly limited. (*See? I did my homework!*)

I boldly emailed her back and asked about the list size requirement. Actually, what I asked was, "How big is your list?"

This is a question that seems kind of like asking someone how much they paid for their house. You typically don't do it. But she caught me on a day I was feeling saucy. When she responded, she gave me a number that was 80% smaller than the number she required of her speakers.

Some kinds of collaborations benefit one person more than another. That's just reality. But if you are the one asking for something that will benefit you more than the other person, you need to consider how to position your pitch. What CAN you offer? More on this later in the book.

HOW TO GO THE RIGHT WAY

Do you see the common factor in these "wrong way" examples? Most of them miss the mark in terms of relationship. They are very one-sided and also very short-sighted.

Yet much of the advice out there is like this. It also typically focuses on growing your platform by reaching out to someone with a bigger platform. *Get in front of their audience to grow your own!*

This book, in some ways, is a book of manners. I'll share some best practices for reaching out and forming partnerships of varying kinds, as well as what I think is the best kind of mindset to have when you are collaborating.

I want to provide a framework for what I would call non-smarmy collaborations and connections with other people. The first part of this book will talk about ways to do this well and the second part will give super specific examples of ways you might partner with people. I collaborated with a number of writers, bloggers, influencers, and professionals to get their tips for specific types of partnerships. (*See what I did there? Collaborating in a book about collaborations. HOW META!*)

I feel strongly that we don't grow in a vacuum. We need other people to grow and find success. We need to connect with readers and fans. We need people who have been there before to help guide us along the way. We need people in similar places so we can storm the gate together and share what we learn along the way. We need to be giving back and helping other people who are where we were a few years ago.

If you are building your platform by simply using other people, you're doing it wrong.

Don't forget to check out the terrible pitches in the bonus content: http://createifwriting.com/collabbonus

2

Why We Need Creative Collaborations

When I started blogging in 2005, I didn't read a lot of blogs. I thought it was narcissistic to assume other people would want to read your personal stories. (I would never have believed that people now post every single thing they do not only on blogs but social media!)

My first blog was literally for my family and friends. I didn't write much, but posted photos of our time living in Greensboro, North Carolina while I got my MFA. I started a new blog when we moved back to Houston in 2007 and I got pregnant for the first time. My blog was, again, for my family. I thought I'd share pictures of my baby bump and share why I was trying for a home birth (*since everyone thought that was nuts and I didn't want to have the same conversations again and again*).

By 2013 my blog had taken over all my free time. Because I cut my teeth reading gossip blogs, I posted like 3-5 times PER DAY.

I did not edit.

I did not plan.

I did not share on social media.

I did not have images for most of my blog posts.

I just wrote what I felt like writing and hit publish. The end.

That fall I went to my first ever blog conference, Blog Elevated *(http://www.blogelevated.com)*. It was only when I heard from other bloggers and began making connections that I began to really grow and see results. By 2015 I went from under 10k pageviews a month to over 100k pageviews a month.

This was directly and indirectly a result of the connections I had with others.

I directly learned about blogging best practices from other bloggers. I started taking better photos and utilizing Pinterest, Twitter, and Facebook to share my posts. I joined a small collective of other bloggers. We shared each other's posts, asked and answered questions, and offered support.

Indirectly, I started paying attention to what other people were doing and the blogging community as a whole. In a few months of connecting with other bloggers, I learned more than I had in the years before.

When you work in a vacuum, you miss the opportunities to learn from others, to give back, and also to reach new audiences.

Other people sharpen us. We get new ideas and inspirations. We hear about pitfalls to avoid or new things to try that we might never have thought of ourselves. Working together makes us better and pushes us forward further and faster.

WHY PEOPLE AVOID MAKING CONNECTIONS

Though most people wouldn't guess it, I'm a massive introvert. "But you're not shy!" people say when I tell them I'm an introvert. Nope! I'm not shy.

But being an introvert or extrovert isn't about being shy or not shy. It centers on where you get your energy. I'm unafraid to interview strangers on my podcast or online for virtual summits. I can make small talk at conferences and love to make people laugh. If you hand me a microphone at an event and tell me to give a speech, I'll hop to it without blinking.

What people don't see is the sheer number of hours totally alone I require to do all those things. Being with people, even sometimes online, exhausts me.

I think that for other introverts like me, especially ones who are introverts and also are shy, connecting with other people is terrifying or exhausting. Or, at best, something you don't feel like doing so you don't. Even for extroverts it can be tiring and extra work.

Some people are afraid to approach others for the first time. It's simply out of their comfort zone, even in the form of email or online. It can also be hard to get started when you're used to working alone. You look around and everyone seems to already have their tribes and their groups and connections. It's like your first day of school at lunchtime, where everyone has their table and you're standing in the doorway with your lunch tray.

But if we want to reap the benefits, we have to move beyond what holds us back.

HOW TO PUSH PAST THE EXCUSES

In college I literally dropped out of our entire education department and decided NOT to be a teacher because of group projects.

I'm sure this story will be familiar to some, but I was the person who ended up writing the entire group paper the night before it was due. I wanted to get an A and it was like people could SMELL that on me. So they would show up with half or even none of their work done, I would do the entire thing, and we would all get As.

After complaining to my professors multiple times, I couldn't take it. They told me that in no uncertain terms, the education department worked within a collaborative framework. Which is to say: I would be doing group projects throughout my classes. Even though I was over halfway through the program, I could not stomach any more "collaborative" work.

I still love teaching and love doing this now online through courses and in my community. But this experience and others like it made me really hesitant to form any significant partnerships. I didn't trust people to do their work. Sound familiar?

I had to get over it. And so do you.

If you really want to grow and see success at building your platform, you have to move past your reasons. You might, like I did, have serious and valid concerns. That doesn't mean you can't address them. We'll talk about how to protect yourself in Chapter 7.

I'm not saying that you should try every idea from the second part of this book or collaborate willy nilly with everyone. (*YOU get a collaboration! And YOU get a collaboration! YOU ALL GET COLLABORATIONS!*)

But you should get past your excuses to form connections that will be meaningful and impactful to you.

Common Excuses & Solutions

I don't have time.

This is a huge one for me! I have five kids and no full-time childcare. Yes, working with other people can slow you down. But it can also help you get where you're going faster.

I'm an introvert/I'm shy/I don't like people/I'm afraid.

You can choose to let these tendencies define you or you can choose to get a little uncomfortable and do something brave.

I don't know any other people in my space.

Are you using social media? This is a quick one to remedy. The first writer's group I started on Facebook was six people large, all women who answered a random call I put out on Twitter of all places. If you are on social media, there are already groups that you can join to start connecting with others. You can also attend conferences or other live events.

No one will want to work with me.

Maybe you won't get a yes right now if you pitch a collaboration with a famous writer or blogger. But at the least, you can find some people in a similar space and form some partnerships. We'll talk about levels of commitment in the next chapter.

I'm not sure where to start.

Great! Keep reading. By the time you finish this book, you'll have a lot of ideas and practical tools.

3

Let's Talk Levels

Before we get into what I like to call the attitude of asks, I'm going to address something super important to the premise of this book. I touched on this briefly in the intro, but the common advice about collaborating online seems primarily concerned with reaching out to someone bigger than you so that you can gain access to his or her platform to grow your own.

This advice makes sense, right? It can be very effective. But it can also be really...gross. I've heard stories and seen firsthand how other people can do this in a way that leaves you feeling very used. We'll talk more about the attitude behind this in the next chapter, but for now, I want to talk about the different kinds of partnerships and collaborations you can make.

A Note about Size:

I'm talking here about people who are "bigger" or "smaller" or "at the same level," but often these things are kind of fluid. I know people making 7 figures who have a fraction of the Twitter followers I do. On the surface (*at least of Twitter*), who looks "bigger"?

Influence can be hard to measure and some metrics, like email followers, are hard to see at all. And others, like blog comments, may not be the result of a ton of followers, but rather being a part of a group that agrees to comment on each other's blog posts to make the posts have more social authority.

Just know that I'm using these terms rather loosely.

REACHING UP

This is when you reach out to someone who is ahead of you, whether that's degree of experience or size of platform. They have more influence or more audience or perhaps more social authority.

The Pros

When you are just getting started especially, it can be hard to gain momentum. If you can connect with someone who is at a higher level, the thought is that you will be seen by their audience or that some of their great influence will rub off on you. You may also gain subscribers or followers when you get in front of larger audience.

The Cons

This doesn't always work, however. Just ask any podcaster who thought getting A-list guests would mean skyrocketing downloads.

It CAN mean that, but doesn't guarantee it. I found that my most popular podcast episodes were not the ones where I got people like Darren Rowse of Problogger or Melyssa Griffin or Aaron Mahnke of Lore. The episodes with the highest number of downloads were the shows where I flew solo.

It's also very easy to appear *(or BE)* smarmy. You might burn bridges by simply trying to use other people for your growth. People with bigger platforms expect to have constant pitches. If you do approach someone above you for a partnership of some kind, you want to stand out as the person who did this differently.

REACHING ACROSS

This is when you are reaching out to the people who are at the same or similar level to you. Whether that's in terms of where you are in your business or blog or how many followers you have or the kinds of struggles.

The Pros

Some of my best online friends and partners are people that I started with when we were on the same level. You understand each other well and know what the other person is going through. You might have unique insight to help each other. And I purposefully used the past tense because maybe in a year, one of you will be that power influencer. Or you both will. You never know where you'll end up, but it's really great to start with partnerships with others who are on a similar level as you.

The Cons

If you are all at the same or similar level, you may all be struggling with the same exact thing and not have a solution. Or maybe you don't have the collective experience to solve a particular problem or move to the next level.

REACHING BACK

This is when you are reaching "down" to people who are where you were a few years or a few steps ago. If you offer courses or services like coaching, often this is where you find your students and customers. But I don't just mean for paid profit, just like I wouldn't recommend trying to simply use the people who are ahead of you for your own gain.

The Pros

I don't believe in karma. But I do think in an online sense, being generous DOES come back to you. It builds trust. It builds your reputation. It builds your connections. Plus, we don't just learn and grow from people ahead and the same as us. I have learned some really great things from my community, even as they learn from me.

When you don't feel like you can learn something from someone who is "below" or "behind" you, it's time to rethink your attitude. There is something to be said for doing something for someone else that you hope someone else would do for you. You may also turn followers into raving fans by being generous with them.

The Cons

I think one of the reasons people don't think of doing this (*for free, anyway*) is because of the time suck. We are all busy. We all have full plates. Helping someone who is a few steps behind you may not have an immediate benefit. And when you don't have a lot of time, this can seem like a waste of a precious resource.

I think at any given time, it's important to have a mix of these three levels of partnership.

When you are doing something with someone a few steps ahead, you might get in front of a new audience and gain more followers faster.

When you work with people at the same level, you can commiserate and share what is working right now. Hopefully you can all level up together.

When you are working with people who are a few steps behind, you may not see immediate benefits, but you are building a great reputation. I think it's also good for your character.

MATTERS OF COMMITMENT

I still vividly remember getting a yes from someone who was a much bigger blogger. I was ecstatic! But I'm an ideas person and immediately thought of the next five things that this person would be PERFECT for. After all, he already said yes once, right?

Guess who politely declined any and all further partnerships? Yep. You guessed it.

When you are thinking of collaborations, you don't just want to think about the levels of the people you are hoping to partner with. You also need to consider the time involved as well as commitment level for each partnership.

This will help you say no when someone asks you to partner on a project that would be too large of a time commitment. And will help you avoid over-asking someone with a larger platform, which might potentially short-circuit a more long-term relationship.

So how DO you ask? Let's get into the perfect pitch.

4

The Perfect Pitch

If you get nothing else out of this book *(besides the tip to stop messaging me about your infographics),* it's this: The perfect pitch starts with the right attitude.

Yes, collaborations should benefit us. That's why you're reading this book, right? But if that is your ONLY motivation, it will show. If not right away, over time.

And just as doing good for people below you often will come back to you in terms of reputation, so will doing things purely out of a What's In It For Me (WIIFM) attitude. When you are trying to connect with someone at any level, it should be with good motives. You should want to benefit both of you as much as possible.

You can't always offer someone above you a benefit. I've had guests on my podcast where I couldn't do anything to help them. Take John Lee Dumas, who was on episode 34 of the Create if Writing podcast (*http://createifwriting.com/034-2*). He has a huge platform and a very successful podcast. I doubt anyone who heard him on my podcast was hearing of him for the first time.

He didn't NEED to come on my show. *(Hey! A great example of reaching back to someone steps behind you!)* I didn't really have anything to offer him.

So why did he do it? And how did I ask?

You can see the specific email I wrote along with other examples when you sign up for the free Creative Collaboration resources (*http://createifwriting.com/collabbonus*), but here are the core parts of my email:

- I shared what I love about him and his content.
- I gave a very specific ask.
- I communicated why he was a good fit for my audience.
- I used personal language.

Pretty simple, right? Let's talk a little more about these three pieces and why they matter.

Note: I use the term "pitch" and "ask" pretty interchangeably. I feel like a pitch is a more recognized word, but an ask is a more inclusive term of requests you might make.

What You Love about Them

This is missing from most emails I get. At least, the *genuine* part of this is missing. I get emails that start with a sentence like, "We love your content at ________! It's so refreshing to read posts that are _________!"

The problem is that almost 100% of the time, these emails fill in the blanks with things that do NOT apply to my blog. It's clear that they use a template and don't change anything but the site name.

I actually got an email a few weeks ago where they forgot to fill in the blanks in the template. So it literally looked just like this:

Dear_____,

We love your articles at ______ and would love to partner with you!

In case I haven't made this clear enough: the sender did NOT fill in the blanks. He sent me the template itself. It's usually not quite that obvious when the sender isn't familiar with my work, but it's still pretty clear. Either the email reads just like a template (*is someone selling these or something??*) or they mention content my readers will love that has nothing to do with my blog.

When I reach out, I get as specific as possible. I want that person to know that I actually read and follow them. *(This is a good time to mention that if you are reaching out to someone you don't actually follow...why are you reaching out??)* I mention my favorite blog post or the most recent podcast episode or that time I said hello at a conference.

A Very Specific Ask

I've mentioned that I really don't like getting emails about using someone's infographic. But what I like even less is when the sender doesn't even share the infographic *(or blog post or whatever)* in that email. Instead, the first email asks if I'm interested in doing X, but I don't get to see X in that first email.

Your ask should not be a two-step process. Don't require that person to email you back to understand what you want.

You can go over specifics and details if the person says yes. But your first email should contain enough information for them to say yes.

It should also say this in as few words as possible. You do NOT need to send a 1,000 word email clearly spelling out the best practices for being a guest on your podcast. You need the simplest details to get a yes.

Things you will want to include in the first ask:

- Time frame
- Time commitment
- Super relevant details

Here is an example (*of just the pitch part of the email*):

I am in need of speakers for my Email Summit and would love to interview you about writing a stellar welcome series. Recording dates are between February 12-25. Each interview takes place over Skype and lasts no longer than 35 minutes. The promotional period is March 6-25 and I'm asking for each speaker to send at least one email. Is this something you'd be interested in?

Quick and to the point, but with a lot of information. After I get a yes, I would talk about what kind of mic to use, the best sort of room to be in for an interview, what promotion will look like, and more info about the summit.

Be clear. Be concise. Save the details for later.

What's in It for Them

As I shared in my example with John Lee Dumas, you can't always offer something valuable in return. You still want to address this and share what you do have going for you. What's in it for them might simply be connecting with an audience (*however small*) of people who could really benefit from what they have to share.

I've also given a WIIFT that is very basic: I'm a huge fan and it would be such an honor to interview you and share it with my audience. Depending on the person you are reaching out to, going personal might be better than trying to convince them of the ROI.

I like to end my pitch with the WIIFT. You start with them, you end with them. In the middle is what you want. You, me, you.

If this sounds vaguely familiar, it's loosely based on the best way to share constructive criticism: You sandwich it between two positive statements.

If you have another benefit, this is where you share that. Examples might be:

- List growth potential
- Monetary payment
- Potential for affiliate sales
- Exposure to a new audience

Exposure *(getting in front of an audience)* is sort of the least common denominator. We've all seen the meme about dying of exposure, right? *(If not, you can find it in the bonus page! It's pretty stellar, especially if you grew up in the '80s. http://createifwriting.com/collabbonus)*

In rare cases, you might feel like there is literally nothing you have to offer that person. I sent just such a pitch to Jason Zook, the mastermind behind I Wear Your Shirt. You can read the whole email in the bonus page, but here's a sample:

> **Subject:** I don't want your list.
>
> Hey, Jason! I'm a longtime reader and fan...mostly a lurky one. I am working through your course with Caroline, Make Money Making, and it's been so revitalizing. Thank you!!

I have a proposal that feels a little bold and ballsy and I would rather call it that than smarmy or icky, which asks like this can sometimes be. It has the word "summit" in it.

[Still reading?]

I went on to share a few details about the summit, intentionally sharing a bit more than I usually recommend. Ultimately I said that I really wanted to interview him and that, other than the interview, I would ask NOTHING of him. Not promotion, not anything. Just thirty minutes with me over Skype.

To give you a little context, online summits have become a huge list builder and income generator for many people. I've run the Profitable Blogging Summit for two years now and it's been great for connections! But I've intentionally run it a little differently than many summits, most of which ask a LOT of speakers.

Generally, when you get asked to speak at a summit, the host asks you to share with your audience. Sometimes a specified number of times. There are daily *(sometimes twice daily)* emails during a summit with sample emails to send and a leaderboard for how many speakers get the most signups to attend the summit. *(In Part Two I'll give some best practices for summits!)*

You might even be asked to have a minimum number of subscribers before you can be a speaker! This helps the host of the summit grow a massive list...by piggy-backing on your audience.

This doesn't have to be a bad thing! But it can be *(and often comes across as)* really smarmy. It's also a LOT of work for speakers.

So in my email to Jason, I told him that we weren't after his email list. I didn't care if he promoted at ALL. *(Though, obviously, that would be awesome if he did!)*

It felt a little risky. I didn't think he would say yes to a typical summit. I didn't think he would say yes even to this kind of email. But I took a deep breath and hit send anyway. Here is the first part of his response:

Hey, Kirsten!

Okay...

I'm in for this, but only because you were so honest about it and aren't going to ask me to do all the stupid things people ask when you agree to do summits.

It worked! I got a yes!

I really did mean it when I said I didn't want his list. I was pleased as punch to have someone I admire so much as a speaker. Plus, I got to spend thirty minutes one-on-one with him in the interview!

Knowing who Jason was and what he was about helped me craft a pitch that got him to say yes.

(Side note: If you really want to make a lasting connection, interviews can be fantastic for building relationships! More on this in –say it with me!- the bonus content: http://createifwriting.com/collabbonus)

Personal Language

Though I'm talking about this last, it's what runs through the whole email. You may use a template (*more on that in the next chapter*), but you don't want to SOUND like a template. You want to sound like YOU: an actual person.

We all get so much automated email that an email from a real person that sounds personal is refreshing. You take notice.

Personal means standing out. This may FEEL risky. When we first start out, many of us make the mistake of trying to write for everyone. Soon we realize that we are supposed to speak to an ideal reader, often called an avatar. *(Am I the only one who hates this term?)* The same is true in these pitches. If we are writing for everyone, we'll sound like every other pitch hitting the inbox.

Be personal and be personable. Tone is incredibly important. Don't go against your own personality, but at the least, you'll want to be friendly. Inviting. Warm. This is the kind of email that gets a response. It may not always get you a yes, but it will definitely be a stark contrast to most pitches.

So…should you use a template? Let's tackle that in the next chapter.

5

To Template or Not to Template

Templates can be really helpful, but if they are not made personal, they come across as cold. It's also very easy to make mistakes as you copy and paste. When you need to send a lot of similar emails (*as I did when putting together this book*), templates can really save you time. They also make sure you are clear and consistent with your terms and don't forget to say important things.

Let's talk about common template mistakes and some of the reasons why you still may want to use a template.

Common Template Mistakes

Sounding Like a Template

Have you ever received two emails from totally different people with almost word-for-word pitches? I get these almost daily, and this is enough reason for me to say no to whatever they are asking. I don't even need to know what they are asking!

While this may sound cold, think about your own time. How precious is it to you? We all have limited time and limited resources. An email copied and pasted from a template with no personalization shows little care on the part of the person writing. They haven't taken any time to be personal; why should I give them my time?

Templates, swipe files, and specific examples (*like the ones in the bonus content*) should be guides. They are not great when they are copied and pasted word-for-word with no additional customizations. As I mentioned in the previous chapter, the perfect pitch should be personal. A word-for-word template almost never sounds personal!

You also need to keep in mind the context of your relationship with the people you email. The same template may not work when you are writing to someone you've worked with twenty times and someone who may not know who you are.

Make it personal. And I would highly recommend creating your own templates or adapting one rather than strictly using a template someone else created.

Copy & Paste Fails

Remember when I told you that I got the email pitch with the blanks still in it rather than my name? I did almost the same thing when I was putting this book together! Because I emailed almost thirty people about contributing, I created a template with just the basic information. Then I wrote a more personal introduction and gave specifics about what I wanted each person to write about.

Except...I had a copy/paste error when I emailed Meera Kothand *(sorry again, Meera!)* and mentioned that she was writing about something totally different than what I actually wanted.

I realized almost immediately and emailed her right away about my mistake. I apologized sincerely and made light of the situation. She and I are digital friends, so this was not a big deal. But it would have been a lot more embarrassing had I sent it to someone I didn't know as well.

When you already have a relationship, this can be overlooked. When you are reaching out to someone you don't know, this can affect the whole relationship moving forward. This might, at best, make you seem a little careless. For busy people, a mistake like this can make it all that much easier to say no.

Copying and pasting should mostly involve the nitty-gritty details and not the greeting or personal part of an email. We should always proofread, but be especially vigilant with templates. Again, they should mostly be used as a guide, with direct copy and paste used sparingly and carefully.

When and How to Use Templates

Templates can be very helpful when you have a TON of information to share and don't want to write the same thing again and again. They can save you a ton of time. Templates also help you convey all the information consistently, especially if you are working on a project with multiple people. You don't want to leave important things out or tell two people two different things.

As an example, when I first sent out emails to guests on the Create If Writing podcast, I forgot so much information! Like: how to pronounce my name. *(For the record, Kirsten rhymes with BEER-sten. You'll never forget again.)* Understandably, a number of guests mispronounced my name while recording. Even after dealing with this my whole life, I still find it awkward to correct people, especially when we are twenty minutes into an interview.

I now send my guests the same information from a Google Doc, which includes how to pronounce my name. People don't always read this, but it generally cuts down on the back and forth with questions about how the recording will take place and what they need to set up.

But this copied and pasted document is not the pitch. I craft each pitch to guests personally. After they say yes or if they have further questions, I'll send along a more standardized email with information. This both saves me the time from having to write this repeatedly and also ensures I don't leave bits out, like how important it is for my guests to use earphones so there isn't an echo on the recording.

For most pitches, I have a mental template that's similar to what I wrote about in the previous chapter: something personal, a clear and concise ask, and what's in it for them. For larger or more unique projects where I'm asking multiple people to do something out of the box, I may create a larger template in Evernote or Google Docs.

Most people have some understanding of what a guest post or podcast interview is. For this book, I was asking for something specific and needed to be clear. Asking people to partner with me in writing this book might at first bring to mind the idea of co-writing, which has a much larger scope. I needed to very clearly state what this project entailed, so I created a doc with specifics. Here's that template:

> I'm working on a book (as yet untitled) about making the most of collaborations and how to reach out and form relationships in non-smarmy ways. I'm including specific examples of different kinds of collaborations along with tips and best practices.
>
> Would you be interested in writing a few sentences or a brief paragraph (200-500 words max) on ________? I will include your quote in the book along with a link back to your site or book. If you are interested, let me know and send me your paragraph along with your preferred link by August 8.

Going along with my general framework, I added a more personal greeting. The link back was the WIIFT. I also sent this almost exclusively to people I had already worked with before, either on the podcast or through another connection. Having this chunk of information in one place saved me time and helped me be clear and concise explaining the project.

Again: a template is a guide. Don't overuse these. Don't overthink them. Consider using a general template *(like my personal greeting, ask, WIIFT)* and specific copied and pasted templates only as necessary. Err on the side of taking up more of your time to be more personal.

Want some template inspiration? I've got some examples for you in the bonus content! http://createifwriting.com/collabbonus

6

Following Up

You've sent your perfect pitch. Now what?

For the first few days you might keep thinking about that email. Did they get it? Did they read it? Are they going to say yes?

And, probably also: Do they think I'm stupid? Am I stupid?

Followed by: Googling "ways to un-send an email."

Calm down, friend. It's only an email. But these asks, especially if they are sent to someone who is ahead of us *(AND if we really want a yes),* can really consume our minds and send us spiraling into a strange sort of self-deprecating despair.

Or is that just me?

In case you happen to struggle with the wait *(and your self-worth in the meantime),* here are the practical things you should do instead, in order.

Create a Note in Your Calendar for a Week Later

Right after you send the email, set an alarm on your calendar for one week later. This will be your reminder to follow up.

You'll find a variety of opinions on following-up, but I would recommend a week. It's just long enough, but not too long. Depending on the relationship *(cold or warm)*, you might adjust the timeframe. Do what feels right to you, but do follow up!

Hit Reply on the Email You Sent

This might sound weird, but you'll want to find the email you sent, then hit reply to it. When you do this, it means that the original content of your email is visible beneath the new email. Seems like a small thing, but it's significant. Let me explain.

I personally get probably ten unsolicited emails a day that are some kind of pitch. I tend to answer these last. Which sometimes means they get forgotten. Usually, these people follow up. Without the original email attached, I have very little context. Especially for the cold asks from people I don't know. Then I have to actually search my inbox for their original email.

If this happens, chances are that I won't take the time to search for the original email. I'll just say no, especially if it's a busy week for me. Hitting reply is a quick and easy way to keep things in one place.

Be Brief

You should have covered everything you needed to say in the original pitch. The follow up should be one or two sentences and needs to strike just the right tone. Something along the lines of:

> I just wanted to circle back and see if you had any questions about [insert description of collaboration]. I would really love to work with you! Thanks so much for your time.

Or:

> I wanted to follow up regarding the email I sent about [insert description of collaboration]. If you have questions or

want to hear more, I'd love to set up a time to talk. Thank you!

You can be a little more personable or add a little of your own pizazz, but in essence, all you want to communicate is that you have not gotten a response to your email. You don't want to send an email that simply says, "BUMP!" But essentially, that's what this follow-up does.

How Many Times Should You Follow Up?

As with everything, advice on this varies. Personally? I almost never follow up more than once. After that seven-day email, I let it go. I've heard many people suggest following up one more time, a month later. Go with what feels right to YOU. But don't do any of the following things!

Mistakes People Make in Following Up

Sometimes I'll get 2-3 emails in one week from the same person. That only motivates me to reply and say no. You don't want to hound someone or appear desperate.

Passionate about your project? Yes!

Send follow ups like a crazy email stalker? NO.

I also sometimes get guilt-inducing emails, which feel really inappropriate. Especially from strangers, which is usually the case. There is already probably a little guilt when the person sees the reply and realizes they forgot to respond. That's an okay kind of guilt! Don't intentionally try to guilt someone into a response. *(Not that YOU would, because you're a terrific person. But I've definitely had passive aggressive follow ups hit my inbox.)*

Not following up is also a mistake. I've had many of my great collaborations come after the second email! It is so easy to let one email slide and get lost in the shuffle. When I'm on my phone, I'll make a mental note to reply later. (*Because I'm so much more likely to send typos in emails I write on my phone!*) That mental note doesn't always stick with me.

But as the sender, we might attach all kinds of reasons why the person might not have responded. We have plenty of time to imagine the worst or to think that it's personal or that silence means no. It might mean no, but in all likelihood, it might mean that the person simply forgot or you caught them at a bad time. We may think that a second email is really invasive, when in fact it's just a nudge. Sometimes the nudge someone needed to say yes.

Don't miss out on an opportunity because you're afraid of bothering someone! You could be missing out on a great partnership because you didn't follow up with a second email.

7

When Someone Asks You

As I've mentioned throughout the book, I get daily email asks. The large majority are unsolicited requests to share an infographic, allow a guest post on my blog, or add do-follow links to brands into existing posts. Most of these are a quick no. But I also have many that I consider and some that turn into great collaborations.

How should you respond when YOU are the one getting pitched? Because whether it's now or later, you will start receiving good and not-so-good offers. Here are a few things to consider when responding to pitches.

When to Say No

Shady Practices

Before you consider anything else, you need to determine if the ask is even worth considering. You can quickly say no or just delete if the pitch includes any of the following:

- Payment for a post with do follow links and no disclosure

- Payment for links within a post and no disclosure
- Links to a spammy-looking site

A lot of the emails that come to me are from low-quality sites asking for illegal things or actions that will get you in trouble with Google, like payment for do follow links. (*More on this in the legal chapter.*)

In short, if the offer feels shady or the person's site looks like it's low quality, you don't want to align yourself with them. These typically go right into the trash.

Lazy Practices

I also can easily say no to many cold pitches that may not be spammy, but are clearly not really valuable requests. It's a quick no when:

- The person has no understanding of my content or audience
- There are tons of misspellings or a poor grasp of English in the email
- The email is an exact copy (*or super close*) to others I've received

By now you are pretty familiar with the perfect pitch and what it should include. When I get anything other than a personal email from someone who has done their homework, has a clear and concise offer, and some understanding of how I will benefit, I say no.

I sometimes reply with a quick email saying no, but if I'm feeling sassy, I sometimes reply that these are poor practices and they should consider a new strategy. I have to figure that some of these people might be really new. Maybe they are throwing things like pasta against the wall to see what sticks.

When to Say Yes

This is a TOTALLY personal decision. But these are the main things to consider when someone sends you a pitch:

- Your Time
- Their Audience
- Your Brand
- WIIFM

Let's break these down!

Your Time

When thinking about a pitch, consider the time involved. *(Remember chapter two about commitment levels?)* Is it just an interview? Are there requirements? Be super clear about this! You can always pitch back something smaller or an alternate idea. Maybe you can speak for a summit, but not promote. Or you can promote as an affiliate, but not speak.

Author and host of the Sell More Books Show Bryan Cohen said that he would be glad to participate in this book, but didn't have time *(in the short window I gave him)* to write something out. Instead, he dictated his contribution and sent me the audio file, which I had transcribed.

Do you literally have any time at all? What would you have to give up to make the time?

Time is a commodity you can't buy more of and you can't get it back when it's gone. That makes it the most precious of resources and why people often say that time is money.

When it comes to giving other people your time, be sure that you actually have time to give and another reason to say yes.

Their Audience

When it comes to audience, it isn't just about size. I know people who have a meager Twitter following and Facebook page, but make 7-figures a year in the online space. The important numbers (*like your email list*) aren't always visible.

It's more important to know what kind of audience they have and what the engagement is like. If their pitch doesn't share about their audience, I'll often ask. Or I might see who is engaging on their blog posts or Facebook page.

Even if the audience is small, you still can benefit from getting in front of new people. If their target audience is similar to yours, then it might be a really good fit even if the size isn't enormous.

If you speak on health and fitness and the person's audience is primarily moms with young kids, you will find some crossover, but not as much as you would for a blog about health and fitness.

Then again, if that audience is used to that other person being their go-to for health and fitness, even though it's the right demographic, they may enjoy your content, but not have any desire to expand their horizons to someone else talking about health and fitness.

Again, only you can make this decision. But consider how it might help or benefit you to get in front of another audience. If you don't see how it would benefit you in any way, then you need to consider if you have the time to, in a sense, donate.

Your Brand

Not all writers and bloggers think of themselves as a "brand." But increasingly, the idea of a brand is widely use. Think of it this way: your brand refers to the whole picture of who you are online. If you aren't resonating with that term, just consider it as your overall presence and how people view your public face.

When you receive an ask, think of how it will impact the story you tell and the persona you create for yourself publicly. We all have a persona that we create online. That doesn't mean we are being fake or inauthentic, but more that we are editing what we share. It's a good idea to hold some things back and to post consistently about other things. We want the right people to resonate with us. So consider how saying yes to something could potentially impact this persona. For more on this, see my post on branding your writing voice: https://createifwriting.com/049/.

How does this opportunity fit into what you post on Twitter? Facebook? What you write on your blog? Does this person's brand align with yours? Do you value the same things?

I've said no to some big opportunities *(often with people who had a larger platform than me)* because I didn't like the way that person handled sales. Or because they sent affiliate links without disclosing them.

It can make your no really easy when you realize that partnering with that person's brand may dilute your own. It may send a signal to people that you aren't who you say you are, or confuse the story that you're telling your audience about yourself.

WIIFM

I've written about how you need to present a WIIFT when you pitch. Now it's time to think about WIIFM: What's in it for me? There may be some tangible or intangible benefits. Perhaps you had a goal of speaking at a summit or writing a guest post for a particular site.

You can also ask if you can do something to build on the opportunity. When you guest post or are a guest on a podcast for example, it's a great idea to ask the person if you can include a freebie or content upgrade. This could potentially grow your list in addition to getting you in front of new people.

(Note: I've heard a few people say that the blogger then asked for all those email addresses. No. That's not how this works. You can kindly say that or just say no altogether. I would not recommend ever sharing email addresses like that unless it's clear the person is opting into TWO lists.)

Be creative in thinking about how you might make the most of an opportunity to collaborate.

Paying It Forward

Just as you need to be careful of your attitude when pitching someone else, it's important to consider your response to these asks. Learning to protect your time and yourself is invaluable. But when you get asks from other people, you should also consider if this would be a good opportunity for you to give back and add value to someone else.

If those people who were a few steps ahead of you all said no, would you be where YOU are today?

You cannot (*and should not*) say yes to everything! But be as generous as other people have been with you. You can't be generous with everyone, but do for one what you wish you could do for all. Don't always say no. Choose times where you can be generous, even if there isn't anything in it for you.

And if it's a no? Be kind. Be gracious.

I've had some really crummy responses from people. These stick with you and start to build a bad reputation. People talk. You don't want them talking about how much of a jerk you were. Especially considering influence isn't static.

As an example of this, one of my favorite bands, Guster, had a lot of opening acts over the years. One of which was a guy who wrote songs and played guitar…named John Mayer. A few years later, Guster opened for John Mayer. If they had treated him poorly when he was their opening act, I doubt he would have returned the favor, which got them in front of a MUCH larger audience.

You don't want to burn bridges. It's possible to say no and still keep a door open and your reputation good.

Think Long Term

The last thing to think about when it comes to partnering with someone else is this: how will you feel about this in a year's time?

You can't always answer that, but it has definitely helped me with some sponsored post partnerships that sounded good in a month that I needed money...until I realized that I would still have that "sponsored by" disclosure at the top of the post the next year. And the year after. Was it worth it?

Make your collaborations count. Consider beneficial partnerships that will have lasting impact for you, the other person, and the audience.

8

Legal Concerns

Though it's not the sexiest topic, you need to consider the legal side of things. For many of your partnerships, you may not think this matters, but I would urge you to consider thinking about this MORE, not less.

Why? I'll talk more in the next chapter about when collaborations go awry, but for now I'll simply say that things don't always go according to plan. And when it comes to working together, you really need to know who owns or has control over the content of the partnership.

Easy Legal (and Other) Pitfalls to Avoid

I briefly touched on this when talking about spammy pitches to avoid, but I want to go into a little more detail about some of the legal (*and other important*) pitfalls that you want to steer clear of. These are very common, which is why I want to highlight them!

Lack of Disclosure

I am a huge nut about disclosure. But guess what? So is the FTC. That's Federal Trade Commission, in case you were unsure. They require clear and conspicuous disclosure of a beneficial relationship.

This means if someone offers you money or product in exchange for a review, post on a blog, or social plug, you MUST make this clear. Taylor Bradford interviewed a rep from the FTC on the Boss Girl Creative podcast where you can learn a lot about what this looks like. *(Read or listen here: https://www.bossgirlcreative.com/episode-120-disclosures-an-interview-with-the-ftc/)*

To keep it simple, you should disclose near the beginning of your post, before the outbound link, and must use ad or sponsored. (*Hashtag optional.*) Don't use things like #spon or #aff and definitely don't leave the disclosure out! A sitewide disclosure on your blog does not cut it, nor does a link to a disclosure page without explaining clearly on each page with an affiliate link.

Not only does this break the law, it breaks the trust of your readers. Whenever I'm asked to do something without disclosure (*because, yes, this happens*), it's an easy NO. Whatever payment you get, it's likely less than the $40k fines from the FTC.

Do Follow Links

There are two kinds of links online- do follow and no follow. I'm not super tech-y (*and I'm guessing neither are you*), so I'll keep this simple: no follow links are a way of telling Google that you were paid or have a relationship with the site you are linking to. Do follow links help your search engine optimization (SEO) by strengthening your site's reputation to Google.

But paid links *(like affiliate links or links from a sponsored post to the sponsor)* need to be no follow links. You can do this on your blog by using something like the Ultimate Nofollow plugin for Wordpress or by adding the code rel="no follow" into your html. This is important to think about when you get pitches asking for backlinks or when you partner for guest posts.

There is debate about how Google feels about guest posts and do/no follow links. This post from Ramsay Taplin of Blog Tyrant shares some of the complexities: https://www.blogtyrant.com/stop-guest-blogging/. My personal take is that if you are writing high quality posts for high quality sites or are a high quality site taking high quality posts, you don't have to no follow everything. Some people take the opposite approach and no follow everything.

What does that mean for the average person (*whose eyes may have glazed over in that paragraph*)? No follow links won't change the fact that actual people can click through to find your site, they just send a message to Google and its robots. If you want to err on the side of not angering Google, you may want to no follow guest post links. And absolutely say no to pitches that ask for a paid do follow backlink.

Actual Legal Recommendations from a Lawyer

For years as a podcaster, I've heard that the content we record belongs to us, not the person we are interviewing. At Podcast Movement this year, we found out that is not the case. Doh! You don't want to find out after the fact that you don't own rights to content that you thought you did. We all care about our intellectual property, so when it comes to collaborations, you want to be extra careful.

I consulted one of my favorite legal people, Danielle Liss of Businessese and Hashtag Legal (*https://www.hashtag-legal.com/*) to find out what we need to know. Here is what Danielle had to say about the legal aspect of collaborations:

> Congratulations on your collaboration plans! The next step should be to get it in writing. Yes, we want you to memorialize the details in a contract.
>
> No, wait. Don't go!
>
> We know the thought of dealing with contracts (and, ugh, legalese) makes some people want to run and hide. But we're here to say that it doesn't have to be that way. We want to give you a few tips to make contracts a little easier.
>
> First, let's address the biggest question: when do you need to get a contract? Our easy answer: get it in writing. Every. Single. Time.
>
> We recommend getting contracts whenever you are exchanging something of value. The most obvious example is

when you are exchanging or receiving cash for certain products or services. However, if you are exchanging services for other services, it is still important to outline the terms of the agreement.

For example, if you are providing Pinterest management in exchange for copywriting, you need to know exactly what is expected of each party. The safest way to ensure that everyone knows what to expect is to create a contract between the parties.

Here are a few terms that you should include in your contracts:

- Payment provisions – when it comes to payments, make sure you specifically list:
- What do you have to do to get paid (e.g., do you need to submit an invoice? What action on your part triggers that you should be paid?)
- How you are getting paid (e.g., will you receive a check or an electronic payment?)
- When you are getting paid (e.g., is it net 30, which means you'll be paid within 30 days from the time you invoice)
- Termination clause – can the parties terminate the contract? If so, what needs to be done.
- Confidentiality – what information is deemed confidential by the parties to the contract
- Ownership of Deliverables – If you or the other party is creating something original, who owns that content? This is extremely important for content creators, so make sure this is specific.
- Scope of work – Make sure both parties know what deliverables they are responsible for. What is it that you need to do in order to fulfill the agreement.

To make contracts easier, you may want to consider creating a template for the collaborators you tend to work with most. We recommend getting electronic signatures to simplify the process. (We personally use DigiSigner.)

To connect with Danielle, check out: http://businessese.com or http://hashtag-legal.com

If you think that these legal bits from Danielle are good ideas, but not something you need to worry about, keep reading. Because now it's time to get into the horror stories of collaborations gone awry. Pull up your easy chair and get out some popcorn.

9

When Collaborations Go South

I've already shared my experience with group work in college and how I dropped out of an entire department because of that. Many of us share those kinds of fears. And while I have seen the power of creative collaborations firsthand, I have also been burned, baby.

I don't want to scare you and I don't just want to revel in horror stories. (*Though there's kind of a sick satisfaction in reading them, right?? Or maybe that's just me…*) I'll share just a few for good measure and then what to do when things don't go according to plan.

GETTING BURNED

Though so many have been positive, I've had a range of not-so-great experiences in the blogging world. Here are a few that I think will be helpful to share because they are very common.

Working for an Exchange of Goods, Not Money

I work with people one-on-one to help them with their blog, social media, and email list. This is paid work, but every so often, I'll agree to do something in exchange for something that could make an impact. An example might be someone pinning some of my content to a huge board or sharing links on a large Facebook page. I've also worked for free with people when starting out in exchange for recommendations to their audience.

This CAN be very beneficial, but more than once, I've done the work but never gotten the benefit. Which means…I worked for free.

Guest Posts That Stink

I love guest posts. They can be super effective! But all guest posts aren't treated equally. I've done guest posts for big blogs that had almost no return, either because the person never shared the post or did weird things like leaving out paragraph breaks or images. It's super frustrating to give up good content you could use on your blog only to have someone else treat it poorly.

People Stealing Content

This is crazy common online. (*It's also very common to think someone might have copied you because there really is nothing new under the sun on the internet.*) Every so often sites pop up that literally scrape content from hundreds of bloggers to create a site and run ads.

What's worse is when you actually know or have a relationship with someone who rips off your content. I witnessed this happen in a bloggers group where, on the share day, two bloggers shared literally the same post from two different blogs. One was written earlier in the year while the other had been shared the week before. Aside from a few minor changes, the posts were identical.

You have to get used to the idea that someone will steal your content, or create something suspiciously familiar. It stinks, but it happens.

BlogFade

In podcasting there is a common term when you don't keep up your podcast: podfade. The same thing can happen over time to blogging relationships. Sometimes it's a gradual slow fade, but other times it's more of a break-up and can get ugly.

Remember how in junior high, one of your friends might leave your lunch table if invited to sit with the more popular kids? That can happen in blogging. Maybe you have a bestie who suddenly skyrockets…and leaves you behind.

Whether it's active or passive, it can really sting! And sometimes even lead to sullied reputations and bad blood if it's messy.

Mismatch

Sometimes you might find yourself in the situation where you commit to something more long-term before you know a person well. When you realize you don't want to partner anymore…you're in too deep. You either have to tough it out or find a graceful way to exit. I've both suffered through some projects that I wish I hadn't started and also had to bow out of things awkwardly.

HOW TO TAKE PREVENTATIVE MEASURES

Really Consider the Commitment Level

Head back to chapter three where I talked about levels. When it comes to a more long-term project, don't commit unless you really know the person well.

Do a Background Check

It may seem odd, but at times I've privately approached someone to ask about someone else. This can quickly devolve into gossip, so I would be very careful that you ask someone you can trust who will give you honest feedback and not tell you more than you need to know. I've gotten some great warnings from trusted friends without it turning into something really ugly, and I've also had people reassure me that they've had great experiences.

Use a Contract

Head back to the previous chapter and reread what Danielle Liss recommends. Where there is an exchange of value, get a contract! This protects all parties involved and in the case of something bad happening, you'll be so glad you did.

Be Specific with Expectations

Before Rob and I got married, we read a book that had a section of super specific household tasks. You were supposed to individually list who you thought would be responsible for each, you or your future spouse. We're talking things like turning off the lights at night, putting away laundry, unloading the dishwasher, getting the oil changed in the cars.

You don't think about some of these details until your expectations (*which you may not have even known you HAD*) are unmet. It's super important to cover the details as much as you can when you enter into a project.

Communicate Like an Adult

Conflict is hard. But we need to be professional and act like adults when we encounter conflict. I've experienced so many people who are either unwilling to communicate or seem unable to do so in a straightforward way without being passive aggressive or just plain aggressive when things get hard.

WHEN CONFLICT IS GOOD

When my cover designer emailed me with the final version, he said that he hoped I had a section on creative tension. I didn't! He shared a bit about how he handles this working with his brother on their music.

Here is what James had to say:

> And when you talk about Creative Collaborations, I think of my and my brother making music. It took us a good number of falling outs and making up and changing the way we worked till we arrived at a good point where we can work together. And still there is a tension. There is still argument and disagreement.
>
> But that tension is a good thing now because it's two strong-willed creative souls both adding to one final whole. And that tension of creative ideas comes through in the music. Things that butt up against each other and it the sum of more that the parts involved. Which is good. We're finding our sound more. I guess when we really get bored of that tension then we'll make a different type of music to argue about.

I LOVED this example, because it sometimes does take tension and hard conversations to arrive at something magical. I can't answer for you when you need to get out of a relationship and when you need to push through, but often we know in our gut if something is unhealthy. If you start to have conflict, see if it is something that you can resolve or push through. This will not always work, but is worth exploring!

You can find James' music here:
https://www.youtube.com/channel/UCpVOBl5tWF538KYnLAgQnhw
And his cover designs here: *http://www.goonwrite.com/*

No matter how well you plan or intend to handle a situation, you can't escape sometimes. You'd be hard-pressed to find someone without at least one story of a terrible collaboration.

Don't let these stop you from partnering with other people! Do the best you can to prepare, try to resolve any conflict you can, and if worse comes to worse, let it slide and move on. You can't control other people, but you can manage your reactions.

When I have negativity of any kind (*whether dealing with people or not*), I give myself a little time to complain and wallow in it. But no more than a day. Then I choose to move on. You won't be able to completely avoid conflict and disappointment. Don't let that stop you from collaborating. If you need a reminder of the benefits, head back to chapter two.

Now let's move on to some really practical things: specific kinds of collaborations and the best practices for success!

PART TWO

KINDS OF COLLABORATIONS

10

Where the Rubber Meets the Road

Now is the time I'm going to challenge you to DO something. I'm going to make it easy on you—this whole section of the book is going to give specific examples of kinds of partnerships with tips and best practices for each. This is NOT an exhaustive list! But it should get your wheels turning.

Keep in mind that there are not necessarily hard and fast rules. Make this work for you and your audience, as well as the person *(or persons)* you're collaborating with. As with the templates I talked about earlier in the book, looking at these examples should inspire you, not create a rigid set of rules you have to follow.

With many of these examples I'm including quotes from other people who have successfully tried a particular partnership or method. *(Collaborating on a book on collaborations FTW!)* The goal of this whole section is to inspire you to think outside of the box and find ways to make creative collaborations that work for YOU.

A NOTE ABOUT EACH ENTRY

For each example I'll share the commitment level and the time level. If you remember back in Chapter 4 I talked about these two levels. The commitment level here refers to essentially the amount of trust you need to have for that other person and how deep the relationship goes.

As an example, guest posting on a site has a low commitment level. You want to check out a site before guest posting, but your interaction with the blog owner could be very limited. Co-hosting a podcast has a high commitment level. You are doing something week in and week out that requires time and money. You would want to trust that person on a completely different level.

If I don't have personal experience with a type of collaboration, I will have less to say or leave the tips to my contributors and their experience. Many of these collaborations have similar benefits, so forgive me if I start sounding like a broken record. I'll try to explain why each collaboration is unique for helping list growth as compared to another.

I hope this quick reference is helpful for you as you look at different ideas and what you want to try! You absolutely should think about both of those levels before you dive into a collaboration.

Let's kick off this highly actionable section with some takeaways from Kami Huyse of Houston Social Media Breakfast:

BUILD A REPUTATION WITH YOUR COMMUNITY FROM KAMI HUYSE

Starting a community is one of the fastest ways to build your reputation and a business. One of the best ways to do this is to notice where there is a gap and to fill that need. The Social Media Breakfast of Houston (SMBHOU), which today meets monthly with 80-100 people in attendance, was one of those projects. The SMBHOU is a community that exists both on and offline, which is what I think has contributed to its success.

When I moved to Houston in 2008, I had a very strong blog and a good online presence but I knew no one in the town. To add to this problem, I live in an outer suburb of Houston and knew that it would be difficult for me to meet people and network since it takes an hour to get downtown. Since I've work from home since 2002, I also knew that I needed to take decisive action to build my professional network.

I reached out to and met with several Houston Communicators with whom I was connected on Twitter. All of them gave some great recommendations of organizations that already existed.

What I noticed right away is that there were a number of clubs and organizations in town that either held their events at lunchtime or right after work during happy hour. Because of my location, and because I had to be home right away for kids arriving home from school, I could not reasonably attend these events. Each lunch meeting would take approximately three hours out of my already limited working time.

I figured that there were many other people like me, as well as people who would rather get their networking out of the way in the morning and continue with their day. So in May 2009, we held the first Social Media Breakfast of Houston at a local coffee shop in Midtown. At that first event, 30 people attended, which validated the idea.

Jennifer Texada, who at the time worked for MD Anderson as social media manager, cofounded the event with me. Also, some of those connections I met with when I moved to town were incredibly supportive of the idea, including Marc Nathan, Ed Schipul and Sandra Fernandez, among others. The event was free, and the venue allowed us to use the space for the cost of the orders from attendees.

Today, nearly 10 years later, the breakfast still remains free, and we meet at Canopy, a restaurant on Montrose. We also LiveStream the event on Facebook, and we encourage live Tweeting with the hashtag #SMBHOU. When the group is meeting in Houston, we generally are trending on Twitter.

One of the most important factors in the success of the social media breakfast has been consistency. We've consistently met on the second Friday of every month. Also, as its leader I have not used it for hard sales.

While we don't make direct money from SMBHOU, many of my clients have come from connections made through the breakfast. Moreover, many of the people who attend have also gained new clients and business relationships. The community members are a huge part of the success of the breakfast. They invite friends and colleagues and have helped over the years to source guests and ideas.

If you are looking to create a community like this one, don't think it has to be the same as others. Look around your market to see what already exists, and instead of emulating, try to do something different that fills a gap. It might not be anything like SMBHOU, and it probably won't. It will be a lot of work, but I can tell you, nearly a decade later, it was the best investment of my time.

You can connect with Kami at: http://www.zoeticamedia.com or https://www.facebook.com/HoustonSocialMedia/

I hope those last words from Kami stick with you: "…Nearly a decade later, it was the best investment of my time." Yes! That is the power of great collaborations!

Don't just think about collaborations. Go and DO.

11

Guest Posting

Commitment Level: Low
Time Level: Medium (*depending on how long it takes you to write posts*)

One of the oldest pieces of advice to grow your blog or audience is to guest post. Does that still work today?

YES! But to be effective you need to choose your sites carefully and optimize your posts well. I don't just mean trying to put in links to your own site, but links for people to get on your email list.

You should also be aware of the limits of guest posting! I recently left a Facebook group because the entire group became SO obsessed with landing a post on Scary Mommy or the Huffington Post. The funny thing was that it didn't seem that hard to do. Every day multiple people were celebrating their guest posts there.

You know what I never heard? **People celebrating the RESULTS of having those guest posts.**

People visiting those huge sites aren't often looking for new people to follow. I once had my Vietnamese French Fries recipe shared on a roundup on HuffPo *(as the cool kids call it)*. I got a big surge of traffic that day and some residual traffic. But that was it. Some people visited my site…and then left. I didn't grow my email list and maybe made a few more dollars in ad revenue.

Then, because the post was featured on HuffPo, it then also got scraped to like a dozen sites who stole my content. Ultimately, the feature did not result in long-term readers. (*And there is a difference between features and guest posts, but I've heard similar stories from people with stories on Scary Mommy, HuffPo, and Forbes.*)

Let's dive into how to get the best results from guest posting.

BENEFITS OF GUEST POSTING

People often have a limited view of the benefits of guest posting. You might think of getting traffic to your site and reaching a new audience. But you can do so much more! Here are four benefits of guest posting:

- Getting traffic back to your site
- Getting in front of a new audience
- Gaining authority in your niche
- Connecting with the host of that site

Getting Traffic Back to Your Site

This is often the primary goal people have for guest posting. It's a good one! If you are just starting out and don't have a lot of traffic, a guest post on a blog with a bigger audience can result in residual traffic for days, months, or years.

But realize that a guest post is not going to be some crazy unicorn that will magically make you a blog superstar. Even if you land a post on a huge blog. I had a guest post up on a blog with several million pageviews a month. Guess how many people clicked over to read my site?

Five.

It's in the best interest of that blogger to share guest posts as they do regular posts: pushing them out on Facebook, Pinterest, and their social platforms. But not all bloggers treat guest posts that way. *(More on this in the section on how to choose sites to guest post.)* Unless people just happen to click over to their blog on their own without seeing a link on social media, your post on a big site may still not get seen.

Traffic can be a benefit, but have realistic expectations.

Getting in Front of a New Audience

I think the best guest posts are on sites that have a similar, but not identical audience. It's also great if you both sell products that they are NOT the same exact ones. Complementary is a great word to describe what you want to look for. Your topics and niche overlap, but perhaps your stories or perspectives are different.

Some people feel scared of this kind of partnership, like they might lose followers. But have you ever followed two similar bloggers or writers and felt pressured to choose between them? No. You might relate to one more than the other, but we aren't typically exclusive in our loyalty as readers.

Every so often you might consider posting somewhere outside of your particular niche, which will bring more of the next kind of benefits: authority.

Gaining Authority in Your Space

Sometimes it IS about the size of the blog where you guest post. One of my blogging buddies Meera Kothand *(http://meerakothand.com)* kicked off her blogging career by writing posts at large sites like Smart Blogger and Forbes. Then she created a social proof banner on her blog that shows the logos from the sites that featured her. Brilliant, right?

I don't know what the ROI of each of those posts was, but at the VERY least, those guest posts give her automatic authority in her space. Consider not just what kind of traffic you may receive, but what it will mean to be featured there.

Connecting with the Host

Guest posting can also be the start of a great relationship! I feel like this is the benefit that people most often miss, but might have the most long-reaching effects. If you knock your post out of the park and jive with the site owner, you might move into a more committed collaboration with more far-reaching benefits.

My first post on Jane Friedman's blog garnered a lot of comments, gave me a ton of Twitter followers, and was mentioned on the Sell More Books Show and on other blogs. This led to more guest posts, which led to other *(some paid)* collaborations with Jane, who had long been someone I looked up to in the space. We moved past just a cursory relationship online and even got to have lunch together IRL when I was traveling.

TIPS FOR SUCCESSFUL GUEST POSTING

To get the most out of your guest post, you need to do a few things. Her are my top tips for successful guest posts with the most ROI:

- Pick the best sites
- Optimize your post for list growth
- Form a connection with the site host

Pick the Best Sites

Many people think that a site with millions of pageviews is the best place to blog. Not necessarily! As I mentioned, I saw very little to no traffic from a site with multi-million pageviews per month. The blogger didn't share my guest post the same way she shared her own on social media. The result was that almost no one SAW the post. So check to see if the owner of the blog actually shares the guest posts on social media the same way she shares her own.

Engagement trumps pageviews if you're looking for results from guest posting. If you want to know if a site has engagement, check to see how many comments each post has. But don't stop there! A lot of bloggers these days are in tribes where they comment on each other's blogs to give the illusion of engagement. You can usually tell by the quality of the comments as well as if the same three people comment on everything.

Check the social share counts on each post, if that's visible. If you know anyone who has already had a guest post there, ask them what results they saw from it. I really HATE giving up a post that I could have used on my blog if it doesn't bring anything in return. Don't waste your time or content on a site that won't promote your post or has little to no engagement.

When looking for a good spot to guest post, you need to do a little research. First, check to see if the site publishes guest posts or has a page with guidelines for submission. I get pitches constantly for guest posts on my site that has never had guest posts. That's not to say that I wouldn't ever take one, but my first one would not likely be from a cold pitch.

Most sites that have frequent guest posts will have a page that shares the guidelines and more information about how to contact them about guest posting. That makes your job much easier and gives you the specifics you need to know. Look for this first!

Optimize Your Post for List Growth

The best way to optimize your guest posts is to link back to other related content on your own blog. In that guest post for Jane I wrote on Twitter, I linked back to one or two posts that I had written about Twitter already on my own site, which related in the context of the post. This led to more traffic on my site for people who liked the content on Jane's site and wanted more.

You should also consider the real estate in your bio. Often people will link back to their blog's main page. Which is fine. It should be optimized to gain readers and get people signing up to your email list.

But you could also choose to link to a landing page with a related freebie or a page created just for that guest post, offering more resources and asking people to sign up for your email list. I would almost always suggest doing something to grow your email list, rather than just getting one pageview on your blog.

Perhaps the best kind of optimization is to ask if you can create a freebie and have an opt-in right inside the post. Not everyone will say yes to this, but if they do, you could use something like a leadbox from lead pages (*which just pops up when someone clicks on a link or button on the site to sign up*) or even embed a signup form.

This will NOT be effective if you are simply saying that someone should "Subscribe to my newsletter." Your form should be fully optimized, customized, and specialized for that particular post. (*You can read my book* Email Lists Made Easy for Writers and Bloggers *to learn more about optimizing your forms!*)

Not everyone will say yes to this, but it doesn't hurt to ask. And if that person asks YOU to share those emails with you, just say no. Unless the language is super clear on the form that they are signing up for both lists. But unless you're creating something together, I wouldn't recommend that either. You don't want to abuse email by not getting the correct permissions. Just say no, or rescind the idea to include an opt-in.

Form a Connection with the Site Host

In all of your communications, you want to be professional, but also do your best to be YOU. Sometimes when we are pitching or even just talking to someone who might be ahead of us, we tend to pull back and be less risky. We aren't as funny. We rein in some of the things that make us unique. Don't do that! Be yourself. Be personable.

You'll also want to knock your post out of the park! Spend the necessary time to write a great post that will bring traffic and spark engagement. Share on social media and plug into your evergreen sharing calendar if you use one. If you impress that site host, it may open doors for a more long-term collaboration.

A Tech-y Note about SEO and Backlinks

Links from other blogs to your blogs are called backlinks and these are one way for Google to see your site's authority and send traffic your way. People constantly try to game Google's system, and Google constantly updates algorithms to prevent this.

For a while, backlinks were a huge place people tried to game the system. Think: Low quality guest posts stuffed with backlinks. People still try to do this, based on the number of emails I get asking for paid backlinks in my more SEO-friendly posts.

Because of this, Google announced that it did not want low quality link stuffing guest posts. People responded by freaking out and making all links no follow, which is an indication to Google that it may be a paid link so it won't count toward SEO backlinks. Then bloggers said to stop guest posting altogether so you won't get penalized by Google.

Let's all calm down a sec! First of all, EVEN if a site made links in your guest post no follow, people can still click and get to your site! It just sends a signal to Google not to "count" it as an SEO type backlink. Don't freak out. Don't stop trying to guest post. (*But also don't be weird and spammy and try to pay people to put your links in posts. Not that YOU would. Just needs to be said.)*

Want to read more on this? Check out this great post from Ramsay of Blog Tyrant: https://www.blogtyrant.com/stop-guest-blogging/

GUEST POSTING TIPS FROM JANE FRIEDMAN

Here's what Jane has to say about getting your posts on HER blog. This may help you in terms of thinking about pitching a guest post to someone else:

> I'm fairly strict about only accepting guest posts from people who are somehow part of the larger community that I serve. For me, that's the writing and publishing community, but I get so many pitches from people who are more closely affiliated with online marketing, tech, or general education sites.
>
> Trust is a huge issue both for me and my readers, and so the guest content and advice has to come from sources that understand and have somehow experienced the challenges that are faced by my readers. Every once in a while, there might be an exception, but even when I feature lawyers, designers, or start-up founders, these are people who have often decided to devote some aspect of their lives to serving the writing and publishing community. It makes a huge difference in how much people pay attention and how they engage.

Find more from Jane on her site: http://janefriedman.com.

12

Virtual Summits

As a host-
Commitment level: Medium
Time commitment: Super High

As a speaker-
Commitment level: Medium
Time commitment: Low to Medium

Virtual Summits or telesummits are conferences that only exist online. They typically have video sessions or interviews that may be live or pre-recorded. Many are free for a limited time with the option to purchase lifetime access to all the videos and bonus content. Some require ticket purchase to see any of the content.

These are a win-win for creators and the attendees. Great content, fairly cheap to put together, and a real draw for people to attend. They also are fantastic to build your email list and can be very lucrative!

While you could run a summit on your own and do all the speaking, a better idea (*and the more commonly practiced one*) is to invite

10-30 speakers to do a session with you for the summit. These people then become your affiliates for the upsell.

BENEFITS OF RUNNING A SUMMIT

Though summits are a high commitment from the host, they are also high reward. Here are the top benefits of running a summit:

- Growing your authority
- Growing your list
- Generating income
- Making connections

Growing Your Authority

When you run a summit, even if you are interviewing other people, the audience sees YOU as an authority. You are interviewing successful people and it makes you seem successful by association. Even if the person you interview is the one teaching, you are still growing that expertise even by asking questions.

Growing Your List

Summits can be huge list growth opportunities because typically the host has the speakers invite their audience. Even a percentage of each speaker's list could serve to really build a massive email list. The big key will be handling the list after the summit. It's really important to onboard those people well if you want to keep them on your main list where you send regular emails.

Generating Income

With either the paid summit or the free summit/paid lifetime access model, summits can be really profitable. However, from the people I've talked to behind the scenes, the summits that tend to make the most money are those with a huge affiliate program and usually a program manager on the back end.

This means daily updates with the leaderboard, prizes for the most opt-ins and the most conversions into sales. I've been a part of these kinds of summits where getting the most people to sign up could win you a car. *(Which speaks to just how much money summits can make.)* Running a more modest, less in-your-face summit is less work, but often results in less conversions.

Making Connections

I have run two online summits and found that the connections with speakers often continue and grow over time. Speaking to someone face to face, even virtually, is personal and can really help you get to know the person more, especially if you have any conversation before or after the actual interview. The Profitable Blogging Summit was the start of some of my relationships that led to speaking gigs at other summits and more collaborations.

TIPS FOR RUNNING A SUCCESSFUL SUMMIT

Your goals might vary for summits. You might be running the summit primarily for profit, or you might have list growth as the main goal. Take the tips that make the most sense for your goals.

- Pick quality speakers
- Make it easy on the speakers
- Be super organized
- Consider hiring help

Pick Quality Speakers

Vet the people you let speak. I know of at least a few instances where speakers at a summit derailed the conversation with offensive comments. *(And I'm not talking about no-name speakers either.)* Don't just choose based on audience size. Go for people who have similar value systems to yours.

If you are hoping to form more lasting connections as a main goal, you want the speakers to be people you'd actually like to collaborate with again. You can't always know this up front, but often you will hear about someone's reputation or you might have some red flags. Follow their content for a while. Sign up for their email list. Pay attention and don't compromise.

Make It Easy on the Speakers

Provide all the things that your speakers need when they need them. Give them links promptly, share graphics, and provide email copy. At the least. Your speakers are much more likely to promote your event well when they have everything they need without hunting for it. You might also consider, as I did with Jason Zook, asking for NOTHING from certain speakers.

Be Super Organized.

People ask me a LOT about running a summit and I tell them this: it isn't complicated, but there are a LOT of details. You can find out more here in this blog post and Create If Writing podcast episode: https://createifwriting.com/043/

With all the moving parts, you have to stay on top of things. You may want to create a project in something like Asana or Trello or a master checklist. It's very easy for things to slip through the cracks!

Consider Hiring Help

For a summit, you could use tons of extra help. This might be a virtual assistant to help promote on social, an editor to handle all the interviews, or someone to build out the sales pages and write the sales copy for emails. If you want to make the most money with a summit, you will likely want to hire someone to handle the affiliate piece.

While smaller, more bootstrapped summits can be profitable, I've heard from people running summits that these profits are much slimmer than you might think. *(No one jumps up to talk about their 3- or 4-figure launches if you've noticed...)* The summits that tend to make the most money are those with an affiliate manager. As I mentioned above, the biggest summits have leaderboards and prizes and daily *(or several times daily)* emails. To get an idea what this entails, Matt McWilliams is a great resource: http://www.mattmcwilliams.com/

TIPS FROM BAILEY RICHERT ON HOSTING A SUMMIT

Bailey Richert has hosted the Infopreneur Summit (*https://infopreneursummit.com/coming-soon*) for several years with a great lineup of speakers and also works with clients on their summits. Here are a few tips from Bailey:

> Virtual summits can benefit your business in five key ways, helping you: gain email subscribers, earn revenue, connect with others, establish yourself in your niche, and bring forth new opportunities for exposure.
>
> That last benefit should not be underestimated, though is sometimes hard to tangibly quantify. Many virtual summit hosts are often approached to do podcast interviews, guest blogging, and more by both their own summit guests and attendees who saw their event. The additional reach and even potential revenue these extra opportunities can bring to one's business really extend the benefits of a virtual summit for the host.
>
> Of course, this does all hinge on one thing: that the host executes their summit well, and everyone involved views it as a successful, meaningful event. To do that, I suggest virtual summit hosts always remember to respect their guest speakers and their brands. Check in often to let them know how the event is going; make them feel a part of your community. Don't just talk to them twice: once for an interview and once to ask them to promote. No speaker wants to feel like you only asked them to take part in your event because you're trying to leverage their success.

Find more from Bailey on her site: https://baileyrichert.com/

THE BENEFITS OF SPEAKING AT A VIRTUAL SUMMIT

I'm going to spend a little less time here, but still want to emphasize that being a speaker at a virtual summit can really pay off. Speaking at a virtual summit can:

- Connect you with other speakers and the summit host

- Build your expertise
- Get you in front of a new audience
- Build your email list
- Generate income

Connect with Speakers and the Host

When you speak at a summit, often there is a Facebook group for affiliates *(but not always)* where you can network with other speakers. If nothing else, it might get you on someone's radar for the first time.

This is also a great way to personally connect with the host.

Speaking at a virtual summit is another way to grow your expertise. You'll get in front of sometimes thousands of attendees that may be your target audience. If the summit host doesn't ask for a freebie *(often they do!)*, see if you can create one that could be linked to on the page where your video interview will be.

Build Your Expertise

As with running a summit, speaking can be a way to build authority. People naturally assign expertise and trust with someone who is a speaker at an event. If the host is someone farther along than you in their journey, that also can give you more authority.

Get in Front of a New Audience

As with a guest post, this is an opportunity to show your stuff to people who might not find you otherwise. Do your best work and consider the audience as you do your interview. Share your knowledge with authority and be YOU. You'll draw in your true fans more with personality than trying to hit the middle of the road.

Build Your Email List

This isn't the case with every summit, but many of them will offer you the chance to have a freebie offering on your speaker page. That allows people who are watching and like your content to sign up for your email list.

I love speaking at summits because the time commitment is low and even if I don't see a HUGE surge *(often it's just 25-50 new subscribers*), I definitely see these as a way to get in front of new people.

Generate Income

Speaking at a summit is generally synonymous with being an affiliate. I've made modest income from speaking at summits, but your income is generally tied to how hard you promote. I tend to stick to emailing my list once a week and only rarely otherwise. Frequent salesy emails just aren't my thing. But they tend to make the most sales. So if you really want to make sales and generate income, stick to the sometimes daily email schedule recommended by the summit host.

TIPS FOR SPEAKING AT A VIRTUAL SUMMIT

Impress the Host

Be professional, courteous, and knock your session and promotion out of the park. Follow up to thank her for including you after the event. Share your honest (*but kind*) feedback and praise your favorite things. People can smell someone who is just trying to brown nose, so just be genuine, but take things a few steps farther wherever possible.

Don't Always Say Yes

I like to say yes to every speaking opportunity I can manage. But speaking at a summit means promoting. You don't want to be promoting a summit every single month. (*And yes, there are likely summits every single month.*) Pick and choose the ones with the most benefit in terms of connecting with the host or getting in front of a new audience.

Don't Schedule Two at Once

I've made this mistake because often the recording dates are pretty far out from the summit itself. Be sure you check not just the dates for the interview, but the dates for the summit itself so you aren't double booking!

TIPS FOR VIRTUAL EVENTS WITH NICOLE CULVER

Don't get stuck in the box of virtual summits. You can create a virtual event that suits your needs or those of your audience. Nicole Culver has been running summits and other digital events as the backbone of her business. Here are some of her takeaways if you're thinking of running any kind of virtual event with other people:

> Building relationships and partnering with people was something that helped me grow my business right away. For years I had built friendships through blogging and supported other women in their businesses. After I started my podcast, I knew I wanted to share the stories of the women who I had watched grow over the past years because they were so inspiring to me. Since I had spent so much time building relationships (*for no purpose besides friendship!*) I had people now willing to support me. For me, it all started with my podcast and then I saw a want and need to dive in deeper so I started hosting virtual events.
>
> Partnering with others for virtual events was the perfect way to showcase my expertise (*teaching and creating content*) and their knowledge. For these virtual events we work together to develop a great masterclass. It benefits both of us because they are introduced to my audience and I'm introduced to theirs.
>
> Over the past year and a half I've partnered and collaborated with over fifty women to support each other. We all have different audiences but we can come together to share our knowledge and expertise and help each other. By supporting each other we're both put in front of new audiences...and helping our current ones.
>
> The key with partnerships is that is has to be mutually beneficial for everyone and you have to truly want to support the other person.
>
> **Some tips for great partnerships:**
>
> - Reach out and start with people you know first.
> - Make sure it's mutually beneficial. *(Example: You're offering value to their audience and you are being exposed to new people, or visa versa.)*

- Be clear on expectations *(if money is being exchanged, have a contract, promotion schedule, length of masterclass).*
- Have fun!

Building your business through collaboration and partnerships is a great way to grow. Set aside time monthly to think about how you can partner, collaborate and work together with other people. When you're done with collaborations, ask for introductions to others who may be interested in working with you as well. And be sure to be a friend and just follow up, say hi and check in on their business periodically!

You can connect with Nicole on her site: https://nicoleculver.co/

Whether you consider a summit or a different framework or format, the power of these virtual events is pretty incredible. Especially considering that you never have to leave home to put one on!

Check out my virtual summit checklist in the bonus content: http://createifwriting.com/collabbonus

13

Multi-Author Box Sets

Commitment Level: Medium
Time Level: Medium to High

I love the age we are in with publishing! There are so many opportunities that simply were not around ten or even seven years ago. Building a box set with other authors yourself is one of those great perks.

One of the ways that authors are using box sets is to get exposure and a coveted Bestseller title—not just from Amazon, but from the *USA Today* list or (*less likely because it doesn't hinge just on sales*) the *New York Times* list. By bundling a few ebooks together and listing them for a low price, it can be possible (*with great promotion too!*) to move a massive amount of copies.

Even if you don't care so much about the bestseller title, it is also a great way to find new readers who might follow a similar author in your niche. Maybe they buy the box set just based on price and the genre. Or perhaps they buy for another author, but read your book because it's in the box set. That's one more way to find a new reader that you didn't have before.

I do NOT have personal experience with this, but author Bryan Cohen shared a lot about his experiences that will be very helpful!

TIPS FROM BRYAN COHEN ON MULTI-AUTHOR BUNDLES

Bryan Cohen writes fiction and non-fiction and has been a part of more than one box set that has made it onto the *USA Today* Bestseller list. *(Congrats, Bryan!)* Here are a few tips from Bryan on successfully taking part in a multi-author box set:

> Box sets are a really good opportunity for authors to use the power of many people combining for one cause. I have been lucky enough to be a part of box sets that I have organized and box sets that other people have organized. It gives a really nice opportunity to see what's working and what's not working.
>
> Now, one of the things you need to keep in mind with a box set, an anthology, or whatever it is you want to create is that different kinds of sets have different goals. You could use a box set as a way to make money. To do something like that, I would harness the power of Kindle unlimited because you can get credit for pages read with a book that's up to 3000 Kenp (Kindle Edition Normalized Pages read) for your book. That means fifteen to twenty novels could get you a significant number of pages read.
>
> I have definitely seen this with the *Once Upon a Happy Ending Anthology*, where we contributed just short stories and were still able to make over $20,000 with millions of pages read and thousands of sales.
>
> Another reason that authors can get a lot out of box sets is because they can try to hit one of the major lists, like the *USA Today* bestseller list or the *New York Times* bestseller list. Now, this kind of promotion is not for the faint of heart. It usually involves a several month preorder period where you and the other authors involved try to get thousands and thousands of preorders and actual sales during launch week on multiple platforms, including Amazon, iBooks, and Nook.
>
> There are many different reasons why you might want to try to get onto one of these lists, which I'm not going to go into in-

depth here. But it can be a way to increase your discoverability and enhance your number of sales.

Now, when you're organizing a box set, you have to remember that the more people involved, the more chaos you can expect. The herding cats metaphor works well here.

I recommend staying as organized as humanly possible. I have seen the use of Google Docs and Google Sheets work well. When it comes to herding the author (cats) around, setting deadlines and making sure that everybody pulls their weight with occasional check-ins can also be helpful.

If you're the person organizing this kind of promotion, it will be a stressful period. Sometimes you'll feel as though you're back in middle school doing one of those group projects where one person ends up shouldering the bulk of the work.

Don't fear, you do actually have support on your side as long as you get the right people on board. Don't always just go for big numbers. You want people who are willing and able to do the work.

I recently watched Gwynn White set up an absolutely fantastic box set in an effort to hit the *New York Times* list. The set did NOT hit the list, but with 16,000 preorders, it's obvious that setting up the right people for your box set from the beginning is one of the best ways to ensure its success.

I recommend that if you're creating a box set of your own, seek out people who have created successful sets already. You do not want to reinvent the wheel here. There are certain things that work and certain things that don't. You do not want to be in a situation where everybody is running around trying to do what they think works. Set things up. Get organized, get the right people on the bus, and go for it. With all of your heart and soul. Good luck on your box set.

To connect with Bryan, you can find him on his author site:
http://bryancohen.com/

14

Bundling Digital Products and Books

Commitment Level: Low to Medium
Time Level: Low

Digital bundles are like virtual summits: they are everywhere! Have you noticed? Similar to a box set of books, these bundles are a group of similar or related (*usually*) digital products that you can buy together for a limited time. If you already have a book or digital product, this can be a really easy and lucrative collaboration.

THE BENEFITS OF TAKING PART IN A BUNDLE

The benefits can be similar to a box set as well or a summit. Bundles can:

- Get you in front of a new audience

- Grow your email list
- Generate income

Get You in Front of a New Audience

Not every person who buys a bundle will download every resource, but you'll have access to a very diverse audience since most of the people in the bundle *(and some others)* will be promoting. And if they like your work, they may stick around for the long haul.

Grow Your Email List

If you have a course included in the bundle, depending on how you have your email connected to the course, each student will be added to your list. I've grown my list by over 400 people from a single bundle. *(It can be tricky to KEEP people on your list this way, so read on in the tips.)* You can also optimize any book or product with opt-ins inside the product or a bonus freebie in exchange for an email.

Generate Income

When you contribute to the bundle, you will likely be an affiliate as well. Sometimes you will even get a higher commission than other affiliates. Bundles are a great deal for your audience, so they are easy for you to promote.

BENEFITS OF BUNDLES FROM MANDI EHMAN

Here's what Mandi Ehman, who works for Ultimate Bundles, had to say about taking part in a bundle:

> I've always been a fan of collaborating with others, whether through community ebooks, link parties, or bundles. What I love best about bundles is that they offer authors and course creators the opportunity to partner with other digital entrepreneurs in their space to provide well-rounded products that sell like hotcakes and earn high commissions.
>
> Because bundles are available for such a short time, it's a great way to really push a high-volume promotion during that sales period and do a big launch without actually having to create

a new product. It's been really fun for me to not only help put these collections together but also to promote them to my personal list and learn from other affiliates during the sales!

Connect with Mandi here: http://lifeyourway.net

- You can sign up to be an affiliate for the Ultimate Bundles (just promoting, not contributing) with my affiliate link here: https://us154.isrefer.com/go/2ndtier/a1248/
- If you'd like to contribute to an Ultimate Bundle, you can apply here to see if you have a product that would fit an upcoming bundle: https://ultimatebundles.com/become-a-contributor

They are one of my favorite companies to work with. They provide excellent training for affiliates on sales in general, not just for their own promos. The support and community is fantastic and taking part in a bundle as an affiliate is like getting a course on affiliate marketing…for free!

TIPS FOR A SUCCESSFUL BUNDLE

Here are a few ways to maximize your participation in a bundle:

Optimize EVERYTHING with Email Signups

Whatever you include in the bundle, be sure that you optimize it for email signups and more points of connection. This might look like a page in the beginning of the book with an offer for another free book. Or having a companion workbook or course that people have to give their email to receive. *(Noticed me talking about the bonus content for this book? Yep. That's an email signup.)* This way you will be more likely to connect with the people who really love your work. They are much more likely to sign up with calls to action inside the book than just a link to your website in your bio.

Be Up Front about Collecting Emails

If you have a course, course software almost always automatically will add people to your list through your email service provider. *(Often you have to connect the two, but your course will collect those emails so that, at the least, you can contact students about course updates.)* Be up front about this in the notes on the sales page or payment page. People familiar with courses expect this, but others don't. With as many courses as bundles include, this can be totally overwhelming! If it comes as a surprise, you're likely to get marked as spam.

Create a Bundle-Specific Welcome Series

Recently I added over 300 people to my list from a BC Stack bundle where I included my Should You Start a Podcast? course. I bought the BC Stack bundle the previous year and was inundated with emails. I even had a hard time unsubscribing from a few lists. (*Which is actually illegal...but sometimes happens.*) Knowing how overwhelming that felt, I wrote my whole welcome series for people feeling overwhelmed by emails. I told people I knew how they felt and would leave them alone for a bit before hopping into their inbox. I got a TON of thankful responses and had a very low unsubscribe rate from that sequence.

HOW TO GET INTO A BUNDLE

Some sites have a call for submissions if it's a bigger bundle like those from Ultimate Bundles. Once you are on their list, they will put a call out for submissions to each bundle.

You can also directly contact a contributor you know to find out how to join the next time, or check out the company who is behind the bundle. When an awesome bundle crossed my path, I've emailed the organizers directly to ask if I could take part in the next one.

Because I've taken part in several, I've started getting requests to take part in a bundle, which is fabulous! *(Collaboration leads to more collaboration!)* I've actually said no because I have so many promotions going on. As with the virtual summits, your audience might quickly get overwhelmed if you are promoting too many things too close together, especially if they all contain a LOT of content.

HOW TO BOOTSTRAP A BUNDLE

You can also reach out to a few friends in a similar niche and put together your OWN bundle. This is as simple as finding people to collaborate with, bundling the products together into a zip file or finding another way to deliver *(like landing pages for each course or book where the file can be downloaded)*. Then you just need a way to accept payment.

These can be great for working together with other people, seeing your name together with those other names *(great for authority!)* and can also be lucrative.

I have been part of one bundle that included five other writers creating tools to help other writers. Two of the contributors handle the landing pages, the payment collection, and all of the back end stuff. We all agreed they would get more of the payout. We split the rest of the money according to how much each product cost.

This was way more low-key, but still earned me over a thousand dollars for very little work of promotion. Because I included an already-created product, it was almost no work at all. I would highly recommend this as a way to collaborate with others in your niche to earn money on products you've already created. You can always create a new product, too! Bundles are simply a great way to repurpose content.

TIPS FROM MEERA KOTHAND ON BOOTSTRAPPING A BUNDLE

Blogger Meera Kothand took part in a bundle with others in her niche and had this to say about the experience:

> Product bundles seem like they're only reserved for an exclusive bunch of people with bigger audiences. I heard from a couple of readers who were feeling dejected that their product was rejected from a bundle organizer.
>
> That's when a mastermind buddy suggested collaborating our own bundle. We'd have more control over the pricing, what we chose to share in the bundle and how we positioned it. It would be crazy not to try it because we already had the products. We also had access to tools since we sold our own products as well. So about eight of us jumped on the opportunity.
>
> We were all in complementary niches and decided to curate a group of ebooks on everything from Facebook groups to branding to productivity. At first it seemed like a huge task:

setting up the payment processor, the sales page, the promotional graphics and the actual promotion. I did actually consider if we got in way over our heads. But once we sorted out the name of the bundle and the price point, the project progressed seamlessly.

Each of us had strengths to bring to the table and a couple of us being mastermind buddies knew who the right people for certain tasks were. Splitting up tasks was extremely easy due to this. We had a focal point for communication - our slack group. Everything, including files, were centralized in this one place.

This bundle was also an opportunity to share with our audiences that they don't have to wait to be chosen. Just because something at the grassroots level hasn't been done before doesn't mean it's not possible. Now more than ever we have the tools and means to create our own platforms and opportunities to showcase our products.

You can connect more with Meera on her site: http://meerakothand.com

Whether you decide to bootstrap a bundle or join in on one that someone else is organizing, this is a great way to connect with other creators and get in front of new customers while getting paid. Win, win, WIN.

15

Forming a Tribe or Mastermind

Commitment Level: Medium to High
Time Level: Medium to High
Potential Cost: High

There is no shortage of ways to work with a small group of other people in your niche. The names, requirements, and expectations vary greatly. I'll give you a basic framework, but before entering into a group, you'll want to make sure you know that particular group's expectations.

The term "mastermind" was first coined in the way we use it today in the 1930s by Napoleon Hill, the author of Think and Grow Rich. These days the term is thrown around by people and refers to many different kinds of groups. I love the way Amy Porterfield defines it: a mastermind is a small, very focused group of business owners who meet regularly to sharpen and strengthen their business strategies. (*Read more on masterminds in her post: http://www.amyporterfield.com/2015/08/71-masterminding-your-way-to-success/*)

Masterminds can be free or paid, but often have a fairly defined structure and required weekly or monthly meetings. They require time and more commitment, but people rave about the results they have seen from taking part in a small, focused group. I added "cost" to my quick list up top because often these paid masterminds can run upwards of $10,000 for six months.

Similar to masterminds, the term "tribe" is typically used for a more loose group that could do any number of things. I've seen these most as groups of bloggers who create private, invite-only Facebook groups and share each other's posts or other content.

I was a part of a small tribe of six bloggers that formed after my first blog conference. We all blogged about similar content and started by picking a person of the day or week where we would share that person's content over social media. Over time, we moved to share threads, and then fizzled out completely.

I've had other smaller groups where we only post when we have questions or want to see what's working with other people or need help sharing or promoting a launch.

Because the terms are very fluid and the requirements vary, I'm going to refer to them for the rest of the chapter as masterminds.

BENEFITS OF MASTERMINDS

I often hear people lauding masterminds as the most beneficial investment of time or money that people have made. Here are some of the benefits:

- Focused, Directed Growth
- Sharing Platforms
- Insight into Successful Strategies

Focused, Directed Growth

Accountability works. This is the reason that so many weight loss or fitness programs have meetings. Or consider alcoholics anonymous. Meeting with others reminds you that you aren't alone and can inspire you to keep moving forward. Masterminds often either have one leader *(most commonly in paid groups run by one person)* or guidelines in place that keep the group on track.

Sharing Platforms

Let's be honest. Connecting with the right people can get you ahead. I think this is what most people think of when they consider collaborations. Jeff Goins talks about this very think in a post titled, "The Unfair Truth about How Creative People Really Get Ahead." *(Read the full post: https://goinswriter.com/creative-success/)*

When you join a small group, you are forming deep roots and connections with those people. Whether they are at your level, a few steps ahead or behind, the combined power of your platforms can really propel your growth and bring ALL of you farther than you would have been on your own.

Insight into Successful Strategies

Despite the sheer number of posts breaking down income reports or how someone did a seven-figure launch, behind the scenes you'll get the real story. Those posts aren't always lies, but sometimes they don't give the full story. Or they represent the 1%, while no one is talking about the other 99%.

People let it all hang out in mastermind groups. They share the truth: the good, the bad, the ugly. You'll find out what is really and truly working and hear about pitfalls to avoid. This higher level of commitment results in more truth-telling.

TIPS FOR JOINING A MASTERMIND

I haven't been a part of an official mastermind, but a lot of more loose tribes. Keeping that in mind, here are the tips from my experiences and from polling other people who have taken part in masterminds.

For a Mastermind Experience, Be Willing to Pay

Across the board people said that paid masterminds *(as in, the more formal definition)* worked the best and gave the greatest results. I've always been a little resistant to paying, but I think very few people can effectively run a mastermind long term on their own.

When you are in a paid mastermind, there is usually a person at the helm who is a few steps ahead. They help keep things on track and manage the group. You have the benefit of access to that person and also the accountability of the other small group members. Having been a part of many groups that fizzled over time, I can imagine that keeping up a more tightly defined group might really be tough.

Be Clear on Expectations

I feel like most relationships, business or otherwise, would do better if everyone got super clear on expectations right up front. If you are creating and running the group yourself, be sure that you guys manage all the details like what you each bring to the table, how often you meet, what happens if people fail to meet, how accountability works, and what other requirements you have.

If you are paying for a mastermind or group, be sure that the leader or facilitator is clear on these. A big red flag to me would be something that doesn't have clear definitions or expectations.

Be with People You Trust

Again, whether you are choosing and running a group on your own or choosing a paid mastermind, go with people you trust. If you have some icky feelings *(that's a technical term)* about some of the content from the person selling the paid mastermind, don't join! Trust those instincts.

When forming your own group, make sure you feel good about the values the other people espouse. What is their work ethic? How do they handle sales and treat their audience? Do you love their content? How might a relationship with that person benefit you? Because the commitment level and time level here are both very high, you'll want to be more vigilant on this before you dive in!

Be the Group Member You Hope to Have

The best way you'll benefit from a mastermind or tribe is if you bring to the table what you wish EVERYONE would bring to the table. Don't wait to see how other people will behave or what they'll bring to the table. Once you decide to commit, go all in and give what you wish everyone would give. Share as you wish they would share. Be generous and kind and committed. This is contagious and will help set the tone in your group.

DAILY CONNECTION AND A COOL TOOL WITH MARIANNE WEST

I thought I'd close out this section with an example from podcaster Marianne West. She had a mastermind experience that bled into even more connection, especially through a really cool app. Here's her story:

> Earlier this year, I took an intensive online podcasting course. Twenty two women participated in this combination of one on one coaching and continuous group mastermind sessions.
>
> Voxer and Slack were our official communication tools. The first week, not much was happening on Voxer. If you don't know about this app, its main function is to send each other audio messages. Voxer also supports text messages, pictures, live videos up to one minute long, file attachments, notes to yourself and of course, GIFs, which seem to be a must on social media today.
>
> All these applications are great for one to one conversations. But the real magic happens in the group function.
>
> By week two of the course, half of the participants had started to embrace Voxer. By week three, we were Voxing at any given time of the day. The group was international with members in Europe starting their day when the West Coast crew was going to sleep. Often, I would wake up to 20 or 30 Voxes waiting for me.
>
> The ideas were flowing. We supported, critiqued, and made suggestions. We asked for help when we got stuck. And help came with advice from so many different voices.
>
> By week five, we had become friends. We knew each other's voices. How they sound after just waking up, when frustrated, or when happy. Voxer built an intimacy and trust none of us had expected.
>
> After several months, this core group is still in almost daily conversation. We have helped each other learn to master new social media platforms, shared new tools we found to be useful, edited each other's work, brainstormed, and the list goes on.
>
> Many of us have started collaborations beyond Voxer. We have created Live Facebook shows, have been guests on each other's podcasts, and are sharing each other's work with our respective audiences.

If one of us needs help or advice, the Voxer group is the first place we turn to. My next application for Voxer is to create an interactive platform with our podcast audience. If you want to join the conversation, Vox me.

If you want to connect more with Marianne, you can find her at: http://www.sustainablelivingpodcast.com/

I love her story of how a tool helped deepen the mastermind and turned it into something more lasting. I've tried Voxer and it really is fun to get to talk to and hear other people from across the world. Audio carries with it an intimacy that the written word simply can't. Voxer allows you to make the world small.

While Voxer ended up totally overwhelming me, it's one more tool to try out with your tribe or mastermind or even any other partnership. It's all about what works for YOU and helps make the partnership successful.

16

YouTube Collabs

Commitment Level: Medium
Time Level: Medium

YouTube has its own language for collaborations: collabs. *(Creative, right?)* You might have already heard this word in a joint YouTube video where two people from different channels are in each other's videos, mentioning and linking to the other. These are very popular and speak to the tight-knit community of YouTubers.

TIPS ON YOUTUBE COLLABS FROM AMY SCHMITTAUER

This is where I confess that YouTube is not my jam. I brought in Amy Schmittauer, host of Savvy Sexy Social and author of *Vlog Like a Boss* to share her insights:

> The people who lose on YouTube are those who assume it's too "oversaturated." The people who win on YouTube are the ones who see opportunity in the state of the platform and

leverage its vibrancy to collaborate. In most social media situations, you're working toward social proof and the different forms it can take: engagement, influence, growth, etc. But it's extremely difficult to do it all on your own.

There's absolutely no reason to recreate the wheel when you can hop on someone else's car. Collaboration is a fast track to exponentially growing those metrics organically, positioning you as a savvy content creator and a valuable resource. If you spent a moment thinking about the creative ideas and opportunities available to you, there is likely some form of value that you can provide to another person or brand that would be a great exchange for a collaboration. It doesn't always come down to how many followers you have compared to another and the sooner you stop thinking that way, the more opportunities you'll find.

No matter what kind of collaboration on YouTube that you want to do—whether it's a cross-promotion between two channels or you're teaming up with a brand for product placement—knowing what your audience wants is key. Come up with a great idea and then reach out to who you want to work with in order to make it happen. Just saying "let's collaborate" isn't enough.

I've also found ways to collaborate with people or brands without even running it by them or involving them in the workload. If I want to feature a big name in my video so they might share it and get me some traction, they don't necessarily have to be in the same room with me.

For instance, I reviewed a book by someone I looked up to in a video on my YouTube channel. But a review alone was not enough to stand out or get my audience interested. So I decided to create a parody song about the book and do a music video. Collaboration success for both of us: he sent a lot of viewers and customers my way from sharing the video like crazy on his social networks and I helped him sell a boatload more books.

Don't overthink this or disqualify yourself. If you don't start collaborations early, your YouTube journey will be a much longer, harder road.

You can connect with Amy on YouTube: *https://www.youtube.com/user/savvysexysocial*

Or find more in her book, Vlog Like a Boss*:* *http://vloglikeaboss.com/*

EXAMPLES OF YOUTUBE COLLABS

My favorite method of learning is by example. Here are a few collabs by channels my family and I love! You can see a few different ways YouTubers handle this.

What's Inside Diamond Ore? - https://youtu.be/A8o_fqHSsYI
Christmas Sweatz - https://youtu.be/at68PMbgyhw
Nintendo Switch Cookies - https://youtu.be/wkPyk04ZEFU

17

Hosting an Interview-Style Podcast

Commitment Level: Low to Medium
Time Level: Low to Medium

I founded the Create If Writing podcast in 2015 and have a number of amazing guests on the show. Actually, I would call them ALL amazing. Whether they have a large or small platform *(and I've had guests of all sizes)*, I never ask anyone to come on the show that I don't find fascinating or helpful.

As a result, I've been able to speak to some of the people I've admired for years and gotten to know others that I'll stay connected with for years to come. An interview-style podcast isn't for everyone (*and my show is not solely interview-based*), but it can have some fantastic benefits!

BENEFITS OF HOSTING AN INTERVIEW-STYLE PODCAST

There are many benefits to interviewing people on your podcast, but here are my top few:

- Connecting with the person you are interviewing
- Establishing authority in your niche
- Getting in front of your interviewee's audience
- Attracting new fans

Connecting with the Person You Are Interviewing

I don't ask people to come on the show if I don't think my audience would be interested. That said, I often ask people that I'm personally interested in. If I want to pick someone's brain or get a chance to talk one-on-one, I'll ask them on the show.

Sometimes there might be conversation before and after the interview that are more personal and can lead to a closer relationship. Sometimes that person will tell you they have exactly 20 minutes starting NOW and you'll have to rush. The interview may not lead to any further connections, but getting a chance to talk with someone you admire is often reward enough.

Establishing Your Authority

As I touched on with virtual summits, when you are interviewing someone perceived as an expert, you seem like more of an expert because you are having the conversation with them. You are also creating stellar content around a topic and bringing this before an audience. It's a more advanced form of curating, which I talk about a lot on the blog and podcast as far as what you share on social media.

You are creating content on your podcast, but by choosing certain guests and asking the questions you ask, you are also curating. Just as you might gather a particular type of painting in a gallery, your unique style comes through the interviews, even with varied people. Value and authority transfers to you as the host of the show and helps people to see you as more of an expert.

Getting in Front of Your Interviewee's Audience

Many people start a podcast thinking that if they simply have big guests, growth will come. And this CAN help. But I've had the most downloads and listens to solo shows on my podcast, where I'm not interviewing anyone.

Still, the hope is that if you interview someone who has a huge following, they will tell their following and their following will come listen to your show. We can all hope! I've actually found that the really big people I've interviewed are SO big that they don't have time or interest in promoting. For me, guests of any size with a more engaged following have the best download numbers. Whatever the audience size, if your guest shares, you can find new listeners.

Finding a New Audience

When you interview a guest, the guest's name pops into search in Apple Podcasts *(formerly just called podcasts on iTunes)* and maybe even Google. Your show notes or episode might start to get found on Google.

To illustrate how effective this is, a few years ago podcast hosts started stuffing famous names into the title of their podcast in Apple Podcasts. The title is one of the most searchable parts of Apple Podcasts, so people might say something for the title like: Create If Writing- a podcast for people who love Amy Porterfield and Pat Flynn. Apple has started deleting shows that are trying to stuff keywords and names into the title. But it shows how much of an impact those names can have.

When you have a well-known guest on the show, people will start to find your show through searching for that person. That guest's superfans may come listen whether the guest shares it or not!

TIPS FOR HOSTING AN INTERVIEW-STYLE PODCAST

While the commitment level for an interview podcast can be fairly low, I would imagine that the time required may vary. Podcast editing is a huge time spend, so even if your interview is 30-45 minutes, there is a lot of work to be done after.

The amount of prep time also varies. I've heard of podcasters who spend hours researching their guest or have a team to do that work for them. I think the goal is to really know them before hopping on a call and asking insightful questions.

I do very little prep because I almost always familiar with that person's work, which is why I have invited them to be on the show in the first place. I do have a template (*which you can get in the bonus content: http://createifwriting.com/collabbonus*) that I send every guest in terms of what to expect, but I have unique questions for each person. Other podcasters ask everyone the same questions in each interview, which can save time and add consistency. I prefer to be more conversational and the unique questions lend themselves to that.

Your interview show can look however you want it to look and take up a lot of time or a lot less time. Depending on the kinds of choices you make for set up, questions, interview style, and whether or not you hire out editing you will be setting up your time constraints.

If you want to start this kind of show, here are some other tips and best practices:

- Practice interviewing a friend first
- Don't just go for the whales
- Try to make a real connection during the interview
- Make everything easy for your guest

Practice Interviewing a Friend

Technology can be a really tough roadblock for some. I started my podcast in two weeks after reading information on the internet for FREE. Yes, my sound was terrible. Yours likely will be too. In many ways this seems to be a rite of passage.

You don't want to let tech stop you from doing what you want to do. Find out what you need to do in order to actually start. Part of that is setting up test interviews with friends.

Not only will this help with the tech, but it can help prepare you for what it's actually like to interview someone. You'll notice things you didn't notice before about your own speech patterns and about what it's like to have back and forth without talking over someone. I learned quickly that I tended to talk too much and that I had a habit of making a particular noise with my mouth I hated. With some time and intention, I've trained myself not to do it.

Testing the actual tech and the actual experience of interviewing someone *(and even asking for their feedback!)* will help you get over your fear and the tech hurdle.

Don't Just Go for the Whales

I don't know where the term "whales" actually came from, but I learned it from the show Las Vegas. The whales were the big spending clients for the casino, the ones you always wanted to land.

Whether you know this term or not, many people are trying to land whales on their podcast. The thinking is that name recognition plus that whale sharing with his or her platform will result in downloads, growth, and maybe even sponsorship and money down the line.

Maybe. That CAN happen. But I've often found that the biggest guests I have don't have time to promote. And they certainly don't need my audience, so it's not a priority for them to share or do anything other than show up at the appointed time for our interview.

Really? We shouldn't ask anything else. If we are landing an interview with someone we admire and who is well-known in their field, that is a reward and a benefit. You will still grow in your authority. People still may find you because they find that person's name tied to your podcast episode in search. But please don't burn a bridge with someone because you really want them to share and do a lot of things.

Some of my biggest shows were solo episodes or people who may not be as well known overall, but had a smaller, engaged audience. They shared and their audience listened. But still, my growth after that didn't take a dramatic upswing, which means that the guest's audience came, listened, and a few stayed.

Go after people who you find fascinating or helpful and who will be of use to your guests. Go after people that you can have great conversations with. Don't just chase the whales. You'll be disappointed.

Try to Make a Real Connection During the Interview

I need to give a caveat before this advice: My pet peeve is other people wasting my time. I'm about to recommend something that could be misused and waste your guest's time. This will annoy me, but also may really bug your guest. Don't waste your guests' time.

But…wherever possible, try to make a real connection. Sometimes this happens before and after the "official" recording. Sometimes you just have a great connection in the interview. You also might get someone where there is no chemistry, no charisma, no spark or energy. It happens.

In order to give yourself a cushion, I like to schedule my interviews in a forty-five minute period, even though I'd like for the interview to last thirty minutes. I am clear about this and let the guest know that we won't be recording at first because I want to check sound and all the things.

What I don't say is that it's really helpful to talk informally before the interview. This can loosen you both up, make for better chemistry, and help move the conversation forward in the interview. Sometimes right after the recording there will also be a brief conversation where I let the guest know what to expect next. A few times, these have turned into thirty minute long conversations and a much deeper and more long-term relationship.

If you hope to make a longer term connection with this guest, these hidden moments matter. But to circle back to my caveat, be respectful of time! If you say it will be 45 minutes, don't go over. Or, if you are hitting close, say something like, "We are getting close to the end of our slot—do you need to go or can we finish this conversation?"

Generally you can tell when a conversation is natural, but not everyone can. You know this if you've ever been trapped in a conversation with someone when you are late and they will NOT stop talking. You may pull out your keys, fidget, look toward the door, actually tell the person you need to go. And still they talk. You could be this person. Maybe ask a friend for some tough love and real talk about this. Because if you miss those kinds of cues in a face to face conversation, you'll definitely miss them in audio.

If you plan for a little cushion and be aware of the guest's time, you can really deepen the relationship. Just don't kill it by keeping them on the line for an extra hour.

Make Everything Easy for Your Guest

Making things easy for your guest starts with sharing what they can expect. They'll need to know what kind of room to sit in, what

they should use to record, how you are recording, any tics to that recording device. *(Ex: If you use Zencaster to record the interview, the other person CANNOT hang up until the recording has processed.)*
You'll also want to provide all the materials for sharing the episode when it's out. Give them graphics, links, video clips—all the things! You can create unique share codes for different platforms with Share Link Generator (http://www.sharelinkgenerator.com/) so that with one click, a Twitter box will pop up or a Facebook post will start to populate.

Anything you can do to take away hurdles increases the likelihood that your guest will share. Think of how you can make things one-click-able. Tag them in your shares, especially if you use something like Meet Edgar or SmarterQueue to share your content again and again. I know when I've been a guest on a show and the host keeps promoting our episode, I feel the nudge to share, either retweeting or just linking to the post myself.

Podcast interviews are kind of a low-hanging fruit in that it's easier to get people to say yes to something that costs thirty minutes of their time than anything else. *(Remember: it will cost YOU more time. But for guests, it's not a huge commitment.)* This lands right in the sweet spot of lower commitment, but high rewards. Starting my podcast was one of the most powerful actions I took and continues to have lasting benefits.

18

Building a Course Together

Commitment Level: Medium to High
Time Level: Medium to High

Online courses brought in over 107 billion dollars…in 2015. With no signs of slowing down, online courses are a great place to invest your time as a creator.

Creating a course definitely isn't for everyone. You never want to do something you don't like or that doesn't play to your strengths just because it's trendy or popular. I have always loved teaching, so I'm passionate about creating online courses. There are many tech hurdles, like where to host and how to record and edit if you're doing video. But essentially, with a laptop and a few programs, you can create an online course.

While courses are lucrative, they can also be a lot of work. Shouldering that work with a co-creator can be a really fantastic idea for bringing in more areas of expertise as well as lightening the workload.

BENEFITS OF CO-CREATING A COURSE

As far as time and commitment level, courses are on the high side, but the benefits can also be larger. I have co-created one course with Angela England of Untrained Housewife *(http://untrainedhousewife.com/)*. It was called Creative Profitability and taught different creative ways to make income as bloggers outside of sponsored posts and ad revenue. It was a great experience, even though we aren't currently promoting the course.

Here are a few of the great things I learned about creating a course with someone else:

- Double the expertise
- Lightened workload
- Increased audience size
- Accountability and support

Double the Expertise

The expression says that two heads are better than one and that is definitely true in terms of courses. You will both bring different experiences and different information to the table. Not only will this enrich your course for your students, but it will also be great for you.

While creating the course with Angela, I learned so much more about publishing and tips for writing and promoting a book. She has some truly ninja tricks *(like pitching posts for paid magazines that promote your book—double win!)* and so I came out of the creative process with ideas and tips as well. She and I both have experience with writing and publishing, but with different backgrounds. This gave our students a more full understand, rather than just one person's thoughts.

Lightened Workload

Courses are a huge undertaking with lots of moving parts. We split up the information but ALSO all the promotional duties and the planning. In hindsight, I'd use a tool like Asana *(a free organizational tool – https://asana.com/)* to keep things organized. You can actually assign different duties to different people and see who is handling what and what has been completed.

We used Google docs and communicated through Facebook messenger. We planned which parts of the course we each would handle and then made lists of all the other moving parts. At the end, we had a rich and full course, but each had done essentially half the work.

Increased Audience Size

When you partner with someone else, you immediately have double the audience. That said, it's important to find someone that has an audience similar to yours or that would equally benefit from the course. I can think of a few things I could teach on, but that wouldn't be a draw for my audience. If you and your partner have a ton of overlap in your audience, this may not be a great benefit and you might want to do affiliate partnerships or Facebook ads to reach more people.

Accountability and Support

When creating courses on my own, it can be easy to get bogged down with the work or stop altogether. I know people who have been creating a course for a year. Courses should NOT take a year to create. How would students ever finish something that took you that long to put together? Often people get decision fatigue or find themselves overwhelmed, paralyzed with fear, or get stuck in tech issues. With no accountability, often the course just…dies.

Having a partner will help keep you on track. At times when I was feeling overwhelmed, Angela helped keep me going and vice versa. Knowing that she was counting on me was also a huge motivator. You also have more skin in the game. If you fail to finish your solo course…only you are affected. Partnering with someone means that there is another person relying on you to finish your work. The cost is greater.

TIPS FOR CO-CREATING A COURSE

As with any big project, there are a lot of places this could go sideways. Here are some important things to keep things on track:

- Be unified on big decisions

- Start with consistent and honest communication
- Maintain clear outlines and organization
- Play to your strengths

Be Unified on Big Decisions

This one seems pretty clear, but because courses have a lot of moving parts, I thought I might point out some of the unique places you want to make decisions together up front. Here are a few big decisions you need to make:

- Who owns the rights to the course material
- Where to host the course
- What payment gateway to use
- How to handle transaction fees, sales tax, and taxes
- Who pays for what up front
- How many students could you handle at one time
- When the launch date will be
- If the course is evergreen or will have open/close cart
- What format – video, audio, written, etc.
- What commitments you make to your students- office hours, etc.

There are many more decisions you'll make along the way, but the ones having to do with finances and the framework of the course itself are where you will want to start.Also consider any parts that are more long term. Many courses have an accompanying Facebook group, which requires upkeep and engagement. Some offer live weekly events like office hours. Others are simply the course itself. Just be sure that you are in agreement on these big impact decisions before things get off the ground.

I want to be sure I highlight the first in the list: who owns the course material. This matters because in a few years, you may not be interested in promoting and launching the course. Maybe you'd like to repurpose your parts of the course and use them elsewhere.

Knowing who owns the rights to the content is hugely important, but often a skipped step. Consider what Danielle Liss shared in Chapter Nine about contracts. If you ignore that advice everywhere else, for SURE get a contract in place before you start any course creation.

Start with Consistent and Honest Communication

With all collaborations, this is important. But again, because the stakes are higher with a course, before you get too far into the process, start habits of communication. Talk about the best platforms for communication: text, email, messenger, Slack, Voxer, etc. Decide how often you'll check in and make sure you are comfortable being honest, even about disagreeing opinions. Doing this first will prevent a lot of future problems.

Maintain Clear Outlines and Organization

When you create a course, you'll have two main outlines: the course outline and the timeline for launch and promotion. You should have a good grasp on both before you begin. I would recommend Asana or Trello for task management and even planning the launch. You can connect Google calendars, assign tasks, get reminders, and even communicate. It's very easy to let something fall through the cracks without a very detailed outline of who does what and when.

Play to Your Strengths

What do you each bring to the table? What comes easy for you? Who has skills with certain programs? Knowing each of your strengths will help you divvy up the tasks and do things more efficiently. If one of you is great at building landing pages and the other is better at email copy, separate those tasks. If one has a heavier load than another, consider giving one more task to the person with the lighter load.

There may be areas you each have to stretch and this can actually be a great place to pick up tricks from your partner. Maybe you don't know how to edit video well, but your partner can create a screensharing video of how to set up the template for each lesson in iMovie. You don't have to only do the things you are already good at, but it's helpful to know these skills and abilities up front as you plan out the tasks and content.

Course creation can be a real joy if you love teaching and is a great revenue source. Partnering with another person to create a joint course can be very fulfilling and financially rewarding. With so many variables, don't underestimate the pre-work of planning, outlining, and setting up communication.

19

Affiliate Partnerships

Commitment Level: Low to High
Time Level: Low to High

Affiliate marketing can be a great revenue stream. Essentially, you recommend another person or company's product *(with disclosure)* and make a commission when someone purchases through your link. Tracking cookies are attached to the links for a prescribed amount of time—sometimes as short as 24 hours and sometimes for a year. There are so many different kinds of affiliate programs and some are much more of a collaboration.

With an affiliate program like Amazon or through ShareaSale, you won't really have direct contact with the brand or vendor. You sign up, sign in, and then copy/paste a link *(again: with disclosure)*. There is no collaboration.

But some affiliate partnerships are actually partnerships with lots of human interaction. Course launches and larger program launches are often affiliate launches with a certain number of partners, an affiliate manager, daily emails, private Facebook groups, and more. There are also smaller scale affiliate partnerships where you might have a one-time webinar with someone else.

Before I dive into the particulars of these programs and how they can be an effective collaboration, I want to take a quick but important detour into disclosure.

WHY AND HOW YOU MUST DISCLOSE

The Federal Trade Commission (FTC) requires that you must clearly state any partnership that has a potential or actual financial benefit. Many people do not know and some don't seem to care about this, but it is hugely important. (*Important enough for me to take this detour!*)

First of all, disclosure is legal. The FTC has made requirements and investigates claims. You can incur fines of up to $40,000 for non-disclosed affiliate links. Yep. That's a comma, not a decimal point. Forty thousand dollars. Not. Worth. It.

Still, some people feel they won't be caught, so they ignore this. But they are missing the second major reason to disclose: trust of your audience. Let me give you a very real example related to an affiliate partnership.

Monday morning you get an email about a free video training. Then you get another email about the same video training. And another. All from different people you have subscribed to online. But it's the same video and very similar copy in the email.

This must be a great video training if all the people I follow recommend it! you think to yourself.

What if you learned that each of those links was an affiliate link and if you bought the product mentioned in the free training, the person whose link you clicked would get several hundred dollars?

What if you knew that the person who got the most signups to that free video training through their links would win a car?

Would you still feel the same way about that video training?

Would you still feel the same way about the person who recommended it *(but neglected to tell you they could win a car if you watch the video)?*

The answer may be yes. You really may not care at all. Personally, I DO. I care a lot. It breaks my trust as a reader. *(It's totally okay if you don't feel this way. I'm a little nuts. I know.)* I feel very strongly that even if you really believe in a product and would recommend it without payment, you still need to disclose if you ARE receiving payment to promote it.

The FTC agrees, which is why you must clearly and conspicuously disclose your relationship. This can be as simple as using the word "ad" *(with or without hashtags)* or explaining quickly that you will receive a commission at no extra cost if someone purchases through your link. Don't use weird abbreviations like "spon" or "aff." Be clear enough that your grandma would understand.

Disclosure isn't hard, but sometimes it feels awkward, especially if you are recommending a free video training. Most people do NOT disclose on those free items, but I would say that anytime there is a cookie, you must disclose.

Now that my mini-rant is over, back to how affiliate programs can be a great collaboration for you.

BENEFITS OF AFFILIATE PROMOTIONS

There are many benefits besides financial to these partnerships, but that is often the biggest and brightest star. Here are some additional reasons you might want to take part in an affiliate partnership:

- Sharing great content with your audience
- Getting access to the program creator
- Having your name added to lists for other promotions
- Connecting with other affiliates
- Leveraging relationships for your own promotions

Sharing Great Content with Your Audience

Many of these affiliate programs have really great free content that you can share as part of the promo. Free books, free webinars, and more are often the entry points for a summit or a course launch. It's in the best interest of the person launching to knock it out of the park with the free content in order to get people buying once there is paid content. This gives you an extra freebie to offer your audience that you don't have to take the time to create.

Getting Access to the Program Creator

Often with larger programs there is an actual paid affiliate manager. The program creator may or may not be super involved. But on more than one launch I have been able to personally engage with someone who otherwise I might never have gotten to talk with. If you want to connect with a whale, a big affiliate launch is a great way to get on the radar.

Having Your Name Added to the List for Other Promotions

After taking part in my first big affiliate promotion for Nick Stephenson's course Your First 10,000 Readers, his affiliate manager sent me an email every time there was a new big affiliate launch for one of his clients. I didn't always say yes if the timing or the content didn't suit my audience. But once my foot was in the door, I was able to participate in many more affiliate programs. I don't think a month went by last year when I didn't make a residual few hundred dollars from a program I'd promoted months before.

Connecting with Other Affiliates

On that same first launch I mentioned above, I got an email from Chris Syme. (http://ckwyme.com) Our names were next to each other on the sales leaderboard. She checked out my site and thought our content matched up really well. Since then, I've been on her podcast and she's been on my podcast and we've partnered in several ways. You'll hear from her in the next chapter. All of these partnerships started through someone else's affiliate program.

In almost every launch I've connected with someone new through the back end of the affiliate program. It can be a great place to network and find other people who are at similar levels who have an audience with shared interests. If you are in an affiliate program with a way to connect, make sure you connect with the other affiliates!

Leveraging Relationships for Your Own Launch

Depending on the size of the program or the program creator, you may not be able to get that program creator to promote your course. *(But you might make a connection with them that leads to more things!)*

At the least you'll have the other affiliates to consider as affiliates for your next program.

This is where it's important to remember back to the mindset of collaboration I talked about in the very first chapter. Don't go entering affiliate programs JUST to leverage connections. That is a benefit, yes. But if your sole reason to take part is what relationships you can walk away with, you need to check your motives. It's so clear when someone comes into a group or program with a single-minded intent to leverage the opportunity.

The differences can be subtle sometimes because successful partnerships mean that both people benefit. Connecting with other people in a group of affiliates is a perk. To avoid being smarmy, just keep checking on those motivations and also how and what you are giving.

Affiliate partnerships don't have to be huge. Just like with bundles, you can take part in a professionally run program or partner with a few people for a smaller launch. I'm in the midst of partner launches where I'm speaking to different people personally, doing single webinars for each of their lists to re-launch one of my courses. It's a smaller scope and very manageable.

You may want to run an affiliate launch yourself. I've got some great tips on those kinds of partnerships from Summer Tannhuaser.

TIPS ON AFFILIATE PARTNERSHIPS WITH SUMMER TANNHAUSER

I've had the most success with affiliate partnerships when I've reached out to people who I've had some kind of connection with previously. We don't have to be best buddies, but they also shouldn't be scratching their head wondering "who is this?" when I email them. I'll normally also include a few "stretch" reach-outs to potential affiliates that would be amazing to partner with, but I'm not really expecting them to say yes. But you never know, until you take a chance!

When reaching out, I try to make the opportunity very easy and not much extra work for the affiliate partner. I'm pretty much going to be doing as much as possible, and giving the affiliate as many resources as possible, so that it requires as little effort as possible on their part. I want to make this a very easy "YES!" for them!

To read more from Summer, you can find her here:
https://summertannhauser.com/

Whether you are taking part in an affiliate program or running one yourself, there are a number of benefits beyond the financial. Don't limit yourself in thinking that being an affiliate or running an affiliate launch is just about the money. I do find them very profitable, but even if the checks from launches aren't coming in, the relationships I've made are still going strong.

20

Podcast Co-Host

Commitment Level: Medium to High
Time Level: Medium to High

In Chapter Eighteen I talked about doing an interview-style podcast, but having a co-host is another great way to bring collaborations and podcasting together. Some of my favorite shows have two or more hosts. I love the banter between Jim and Bryan on the Sell More Books Show *(http://sellmorebooksshow.com)* and love the chemistry on the Fizzle Show *(http://fizzle.co)*. And I'm a total sucker for John and Sherry of Young House Love Has a Podcast *(http://younghouselove.com/podcast)*. I also love We Talk Different *(https://www.facebook.com/wetalkdifferent/)*.

Having a podcast co-host can bring an extra dose of energy to a show, plus have a more colorful perspective. It also has the benefit of bringing in several already-built audiences (*if you and your cohost each already have a platform*) and attracting people together that you might not attract if you did a solo show.

Podcasts have a lot of weekly moving parts. I know what it takes to pull off a solo show, so I can imagine all the details that go into having another host. To get insight on this, I had Chris Syme of the Smarty Pants Book Marketing Podcast share how this works for her.

HOW TO MAKE A CO-HOSTED PODCAST WORK FOR YOU WITH CHRIS SYME

My daughter and I wear different hats in our work lives but we have the same heart for indie authors who are frustrated trying to figure out how to sell their own books. She is a bestselling author who knows those struggles firsthand, and I am an experienced marketer who knows how to find the solutions. So naturally, we wanted to put together a podcast to help authors learn how to market their books, right?

We started the Smarty Pants Book Marketing Podcast over a year ago and both of us are humbled by how the podcast took off. I think listeners like the give and take. Sometimes we play good cop, bad cop, and sometimes we're on the same page. We choose subjects that our listeners suggest and invite guest co-hosts that have resources that will help authors fulfill that mission of selling more books with less marketing. Ours is the perfect collaboration. The hardest challenge we have is Becca occasionally calling me Mom instead of Chris.

I have a background in radio, so talking in front of a microphone was easy for me and Becca has a background in drama, which also helps. I have a friend in the podcast biz who hooked me up with all the right tools and services. Here's a look at what we use:

- Record interviews on Skype using Call Recorder *(no video)*
- Edit the wav files on Audacity *(you can also use ScreenFlow or other video editing apps)*
- Convert to mp3s and level audio outputs with Levelator *(app)*
- We house our shows on Libsyn *(costs me $20/month)*
- Publish the podcasts on iTunes, Stitcher *(for Android users)*, and my Wordpress website

Smarty pants tip: When we first started out we wanted to get off the ground quickly so we made a wish list of people we wanted to have on the show—the sky was the limit. To our surprise, most of them said yes. Don't be afraid to ask the "experts" to come on your show.

Many of them are delighted to have the opportunity, especially if you invite them to promote a new book or product of their own. Just a caveat: we don't invite guests who we feel are spammy, sales-y or just have products, but nothing helpful to say. We also like to visit with authors who are rock stars at selling their books and have found a creative way to get 'er done.

One of the best things about producing a podcast is that it entails minimum cost. We spend about $25 a month putting our podcast together and most of that is for storage space on Libsyn. The downside is the time commitment. My podcast rock star buddy keeps telling me we should monetize our show but, for now, we're just happy to be helpful. And we have fun doing it.

You can connect with Chris on her site: http://cksyme.com

SHOULD YOU COHOST A PODCAST?

If you want to start a podcast, it can be a really amazing way to build your platform, authority, and make connections. There are so many great benefits! But it also is an incredibly huge time suck and requires a lot of tech knowledge. Once you get a workflow, they aren't so bad, but the first few episodes will be rockier.

What I will say is that most podcasts (*as Chris hinted at above*) are not big money makers. I've gone through lots of trainings where people try to sell you on this idea of making tons of money and getting great sponsorships. It's hard. And you need a LOT of listeners. I just want to be clear on that before you go out and start a podcast to make your millions.

Cohosting can make things easier or harder. I know some people who team up and one simply shows up for the call while the other does All the Things. You really need to define that ahead of time in a way that works for both of you. Podcasts have a big task list (*even if some things, like tagging the media file and converting to mp3 don't take long*) and working with someone else means making sure you guys clearly define the roles.

If you are seriously thinking about starting a podcast *(whether alone or with a cohost),* I've got a mini course called Should You Start a Podcast? I share some of my workflow and also have interviews with podcasters in various niches to get their tips and what's working for them. It is NOT a full-blown training on how to start a podcast, but is much richer in terms of sharing intimate experiences from successful podcasters.

If that sounds like it's right up your alley, check it out here: https://should-you-start-a-podcast.teachery.co/bc-stack-page

I'll also have a sample video from the course in the bonus materials: http://createifwriting.com/collabbonus

21

Newsletter Swap

Commitment Level: Low to Medium
Time Level: Low

If you didn't already know this about me, I'm a huge nerd about email lists. *(You can check out my book* Email Lists Easy *for more on how to rock your email list: http://createifwriting.com/emailbook)* Your email subscribers are your most qualified takers of action. Rather than just clicking a follow button on social media, they have taken the time to type out their email address and then opened your email to confirm that yes, they want to hear from you.

In his book *Your First 1000 Copies*, Tim Grahl shares that one of the authors he worked with made fifty sales through email for every ONE sale on a social media platform. In a 2016 study, Campaign Monitor found that email has an ROI of 4400%. That means that people investing $1 in are seeing $44 coming out. *(Check out more of their stats here: https://www.campaignmonitor.com/blog/email-marketing/2016/01/70-email-marketing-stats-you-need-to-know/)*

Convinced email is powerful?? One powerful way to collaborate when it comes to email lists is to try a newsletter swap. I've seen this done two ways. The first is where authors cross promote each other in their emails to fans. I brought in author Jamie Davis, who is a seasoned swapper, to share some tips.

HOW TO RUN A SUCCESSFUL NEWSLETTER SWAP FROM JAMIE DAVIS

Newsletter swaps between authors of the same or similar genres offer an opportunity for each author to find new readers from among the fans of the other author. It is based on the premise that authors aren't really in competition with each other because we can't possibly write books as fast as our fans read them. By sharing some curated choices of similar books with our fans, we offer them the service of helping them choose the next book on their list while they wait for us to put out the next book.

Regular swaps also give the author an opportunity to continue to reach out to fans via their email list on a more regular basis. It trains the readers to expect and open your emails. This improves open and click-through rates on the emails you send for your own book releases later on, increasing sales.

Some authors only swap with newsletters of a similar or larger size than their own. However, if your list is smaller, sometimes you can work around this by offering to promote their book in two consecutive newsletters, doubling their exposure in relation to your smaller list. Don't be afraid to ask and offer this option. The worst they can say is no.

There are a couple of rules to keep in mind when engaging in book swaps. First, understand the difference between recommendations versus suggestions. Some authors prefer to only present books to their audience they've read and can recommend. Others are comfortable with swapping books from established authors with good reviews even if they haven't read the books. Either way, it's important to NEVER lie to your readers. Don't pretend you've read the book when you haven't. One thing I do is say I'm suggesting a new book from an author friend without stating an explicit recommendation that sounds as if I've read it.

Second, keep records of your swaps and put them on your calendar. It is bad form to arrange a swap and then fail to swap as agreed. I keep a spreadsheet with all my swaps on them. It includes the author name, link to their book, their email address or Facebook profile page, the dates we will each do the swap and the size of the author's email list.

Third, report back after the swap. When I do the swap, I check off that it's done in my spreadsheet and I collect data on the number of clicks on their link in my newsletter. Most email services allow you to track clicks on your newsletters sent out. It's a great courtesy to contact the author you swapped with and give them your click data on their link. It tells them you actually remembered to send the swap and reminds them to send yours out, too. This is not something everyone does and it can build a lot of good will between you and the other author. It also gives them the opportunity to check sales on the day of your newsletter and check the ratio of clicks to sales.

Finally, be careful you don't overbook yourself and inundate your readers with so many books they don't have time to read yours when you have a new release. This is another way the spreadsheet comes in handy by keeping track of exactly how many you have running and coming up in the future.

All in all, newsletter swaps are great ways to collaborate with other authors in building larger numbers of loyal fans for your books. Done right, it can also create lasting professional relationships that may develop into other forms of collaboration.

You can connect with Jamie on his site: http://jamiedavisbooks.com

I love those tips and the idea that we can all succeed better by supporting each other rather than seeing other people in our niche as competition. This can work just as well for bloggers sharing other bloggers' posts or sharing similar links or services for other online businesses.

NEWSLETTER TAKEOVERS

Another option for a newsletter swap is to actually let that other person take OVER your newsletter and send out an email to your people through your email service provider. The cool kids are already doing this with Snapchat, where influencers take over each other's accounts for a day or a few hours.

If you try this with email, it's important to note that you never share those emails, as your subscribers only gave you permission. You can give that other person access to your login by using something like One Pass to let them in for this time. Or they could send you the text and then you can format the email and handle sending it out.

There are pros and cons to this kind of swap. Some people feel that it's disingenuous. People signed up for YOU, not another person. I see that. I also see how hearing from someone else can be a benefit and add value. You are the gatekeeper for your list and should take that seriously. I would not do this frequently and I would be very discriminating. You could also set people up for this, like letting them know on Monday your email will have a special guest. Setting expectations is huge when it comes to keeping your readers' trust.

Whether you are doing a full takeover or a swap to promote, this form of collaboration takes little effort but can be really powerful because of the quality of your email subscribers.

22

Hosting Twitter Chats

Commitment Level: Medium
Time Level: Low to Medium, but Intense

If you've never taken part in a Twitter chat, they are a fast-moving group conversation on Twitter and perhaps the very best way to make connections on the platform. Typically, for an hour a week, users join up to talk, all using the same hashtag. You can follow on the Twitter platform, but it's easier using lists in Hootsuite or even a free app like TweetChat where you block out everything but the conversation.

While an hour a week doesn't sound like a huge time commitment, it is a very intense hour if you run the chat. You are posting the pre-planned conversation starters and questions, plus trying to interact with other people. To run an effective chat, you also need to have some tweets prewritten and even images if you want to use them.

Madalyn Sklar is the host of the Twitter Smarter Twitter chat (*and podcast of the same name*) and is my go-to expert for these chats. Here are some of her thoughts.

THE POWER OF TWITTER CHATS WITH MADALYN SKLAR

I love Twitter chats! I can connect with lots of like-minded people in a very short period of time. Most of the colleagues and influencers I know, I first met on a chat. I've been able to use Twitter chats, whether I'm hosting, guesting or just participating, as a way to get to know people who can help me in my career.

I've had the opportunity to collaborate in podcasts, webinars, conference presentations and mastermind groups. And have been invited to be a guest in ten Twitter chats so far this year. It's amazing how much magic is in a one hour chat.

Connect with Madalyn and learn more about the power of Twitter:
http://madalynsklar.com

I feel like Twitter is often overlooked when compared to other shiny, new platforms. People may not see as much traffic through using Twitter, but the power of that platform is really in the connections and the influence. Twitter chats can really supercharge the connections you make.

TIPS FOR HOSTING A SUCCESFUL TWITTER CHAT

If you are going to be a guest on a chat, your host will likely walk you through all the details. Here are my tips for hosting a chat:

- Keep a spreadsheet of pre-loaded tweets
- Create branded images ahead of time
- Plan around topics that interest your people
- Promote, promote, promote
- Remind people how chats work

Keep a Spreadsheet of Pre-Loaded Tweets

Whether you post these pre-loaded tweets in the moment every few minutes or use a scheduler, you'll want a series of tweets and questions that relate to your topic all ready to go. Then you can focus on the interaction in the chat itself, without having to think of things on the spot or remember to keep using the hashtag. Seems simple, but when tweets are flying, you'll want as much help as you can get!

Create Branded Images Ahead of Time

You'll want a mix of text and images in the chat to keep interest, so create images that match your overall brand and preload some tweets with those images. You could introduce yourself or your guest at the beginning with an image, put quotables on images, or have your questions on an image so they won't get lost in the chat.

Plan Around Topics That Interest Your People

Bobbie Byrd and Lisa Stauber host the #BlogElevated Twitter chats, another one of my favorites. Often their weekly chats are on a topic that people are already talking about in their Facebook group. Planning around something that people are already interested in is a great way to ensure that they'll show up and get value from your chat.

Promote, Promote, Promote

Just because you have a chat every single Monday, you can't assume people will remember. You'll want to post in your Facebook group, on your Facebook page, send an email, tweet, and even tag people who have asked for a reminder before the chat. Ask your people to invite their friends as well by tagging them and using the hashtag in the first few minutes of the chat.

Remind People How Chats Work

It's always a good idea to remind people how a Twitter chat works. Use the hashtag, use A1 if you're answering the first question *(or Q1, as it will look in chat)*, for example. Some people also encourage side conversations to stop using the hashtag or to save them for later, but honestly—I think if you're getting people talking, the Twitter chat is doing its job. You can't control how people behave.

Another element might be adding in a guest expert each week at the chat. This is similar to having a guest on your podcast or even a guest post, but with the live action and interaction of Twitter. That guest may bring some of their audience or even new people who just want to connect.

Twitter really makes the world small by bringing people together and Twitter chats can be a very manageable, powerful tool to widen your reach.

23

Trading Services

Commitment Level: Medium
Time Level: Medium

At any given time, there are a million things I could be doing online: scheduling Tweets, updating old posts, responding to messages and comments, creating content, editing podcasts, pinning to boards on Pinterest, asking questions in my Facebook group. It is often overwhelming.

One really fantastic behind-the-scenes way to connect with someone else is to offer your services in exchange for social shares or other non-monetary benefits. Paula Rollo has some great tips on this kind of collaboration and how it can benefit you.

TIPS FOR TRADING SERVICES FROM PAULA ROLLO

Everyone has something they are amazing at and other things they hate doing. Find something you love and excel at and see if you can trade that service with another blogger or influencer to get something you need.

Here are just a few things that could be negotiated among bloggers of various sizes and skill levels.

- Facebook shares
- Pinterest pins
- scheduling Tailwind *(a Pinterest and Instagram scheduling app)*
- creating round-up images
- writing guest posts
- dropping links in round up groups or share groups on Facebook
- coming up with quote images/memes
- redoing old images
- updating old posts with a blogger's new product/sales page
- anything you are good at/love doing!

Tip: If you are the smaller blogger, try to think of something time consuming that a larger blogger might get bogged down doing (*like scheduling Tailwind, or facebook*). Offer to do those services for free in exchange for shares that can get you pageviews! It's a win-win!

Connect with Paula in her Quick Blogging Tips group for more: https://www.facebook.com/groups/1373784316041038/

BEST PRACTICES

If you want to try out this method, here are some things to keep in mind before you dive in:

Find someone trustworthy
Create accountability
Consider ROI

Find Someone Trustworthy

As with any kind of collaboration, you'll want to find someone that you REALLY trust. If they are posting for you on a social platform, they are representing your brand. It won't show their name, but YOURS. We've all seen big flubs on social media where a simple misspelling can have a really unintended effect.

Create Accountability

I've had a few situations where I worked for someone in exchange for social shares or recommendations that never happened. If you aren't going to create an actual contract, at the least find a way to make sure this happens. I can tell you that I really hated working for a few hours and getting nothing instead of something that really could have been powerful. It also impacted my relationship with that person long term. Many times you might have access and be posting the content yourself, so that's easy, but if you don't have the control, make sure you have some kind of accountability or are okay talking with the person about it if they don't do what they promised.

Consider ROI

When you are choosing the services or shares that you trade, consider what the return will be. You may not always know this up front, so if you're seeing that there are no clicks happening when someone shares a post for you on Facebook, see if you can renegotiate for something else that's on equal level with what you're doing. Some things might have more power than others, so test it out and see what works best for both parties.

I love this idea of working together on tasks you might normally pass off to a virtual assistant. Not only can this save you money, but it's also a way to help each other out. I've seen people do this for larger Facebook pages and get huge residual traffic as a result. While I generally don't encourage working for free, trading service for service can be a totally different and amazing option.

24

Hosting an In-Person Event

Commitment Level: Medium to High
Time Level: Medium to High

With the rise of digital events, it can be easy to look past actual, live, in PERSON events. *(You'll hear more about attending in-person events in the final chapter!)* As with digital, in-person events can be a few hour or few day event. Kami Huyse shared in Chapter One about Houston Social Media Breakfast, a once monthly breakfast for networking and education.

Andi Cumbo-Floyd of Andilit hosts an annual writers' retreat and shared a little bit about the back-end of that experience.

BENEFITS FOR HOSTING A RETREAT FROM ANDI CUMBO-FLOYD

Each summer, Kelly Chripczuk, Shawn Smucker, and I do a writers' retreat here at my farm. I couldn't actually tell you how we came to do this together except to say that I did the first one on my own, and it nearly exhausted my husband and I.

A full weekend's activities for any group of people requires a lot of coordination – everything from guiding people to lodging, to handling questions about the retreat itself, to being sure everyone is fed, to changing the hand towels in the bathroom. And that's before you even think about the programming.

So for us, collaboration was the wisest move. The three of us work together to get the website up – with Kelly doing the graphic design and me doing the site building via Leadpages. We all brainstorm speakers together and then invite the ones who give us the most depth and true diversity in our offerings.

Then, during the event itself, we split the duties as well. Shawn emcees our opening evening, and I facilitating a closing conversation. Kelly leads meditation exercises several times a day. We each spend our time talking with participants, and we also try to steal a little time with each other to just connect both about the retreat and as friends.

In every way, this collaboration makes the retreat both stronger and more manageable, and every year, it is my favorite weekend. Working with other writers to do something we all know is meaningful for us and for the attendees, that's affirming for a writer's soul.

If you want to hear more about the 2018 retreat, you can get more info here: https://andilit.com/retreat2018/

Or simply connect with Andi: https://andilit.com

Doesn't that sound refreshing? Clearly an in-person event has a lot of moving parts and a lot of details, but shouldering the load together can help with the overwhelm. It also serves to bond the hosts together as they continue to work toward that common goal. Plus, you don't have to be great at landing pages and images and setting up a site and all the things! Splitting according to your strengths will help make this possible.

TIPS FOR HOSTING AN IN-PERSON EVENT

Because I'm just beginning to host my own in-person events, I don't have a ton of tips from my experience. I ran a lot of conferences and events when I worked with for a church youth group. Maybe that gives me MORE experience, since handling large groups of teenager and travel is already daunting… In any case, here are some tips if you plan to try in-person events:

- Be clear on the mission
- Find a location that suits the mission
- Start with a few core people
- Overplan
- Secure sponsorships

Be Clear on the Mission

I'm a big proponent of finding your why. On a grander scale, but also for each of the smaller things. They should fit into your bigger why somehow, but they each can have their own purpose. If you define this clearly, it will help you make all the other decisions along the way. Think both about your personal goals for you and for the attendees as well. What will you get out of this? How will this benefit your guests?

Find a Location That Suits the Mission

This is where the clear why helps you make decisions. Knowing you want an intimate gathering, for example, will help you choose a location and maybe also help you decide to use something like EventBrite to limit the number of attendees. Take some time to be clear on the mission, both for now and thinking a year or so ahead.

Start with a Few Core People

Your live event will have a better foundation if you know you won't be alone in a room. Find at least a few people that you can count on to be your core. They can help spread the word, but also just be there to set the tone and make people feel comfortable as they arrive to see that there are already attendees.

Overplan

Things will go wrong. Many things, perhaps. I am not quite a pessimist, but more of a worst-case-scenario planner. I need to consider all the things that COULD go wrong so I can be mentally prepared. This comes in handy here. Have a backup and a backup for your backup. Try to have a way to reach your attendees, whether through an email list, a Facebook group, or an app like EventBrite or Evite.

Secure Sponsorships

You'll get a LOT more about how-to in the next chapter, but I want to get you thinking about having sponsors for your event. This helps offset the cost, but can also benefit your guests if it's a brand they may want to partner with. Sponsors give an air of validity to your event as well and make it seem more professional from the get-go.

There are so many kinds of live events that specific tips beyond these are hard. Some will require much longer planning periods and each will have unique logistics. Whatever event you're considering, start with the why. People often skip this, but it could help save you thousands of dollars if you jump on board to have a retreat when what you really should have planned was a two-hour event.

The next chapter on sponsorships will give you some specifics to that piece and in Chapter 28 I'll share how I leverage live events as an attendee.

25

SECURING SPONSORSHIPS

Commitment Level: Low to Medium
Time Level: Low to Medium

A great *(and lucrative)* way to partner on various projects is by securing sponsorships from brands. Many influencers and bloggers are pretty familiar with sponsorships, but in case you haven't ever done this directly with a company, I want to go into a little more depth.

I've worked with brands through companies like Social Fabric and Blogher that act as a go-between or broker. That company creates a campaign for the brand, then hires it out to bloggers. I've worked directly with a few brands (like Imperial Sugar) for my blog, but had the privilege of working with a few brands for the launch of this book! I'll share details from all those experiences so you can get some ideas of how this can work.

Typically a sponsorship looks like a brand or company offering money, services, or product in exchange for promoting the brand in some fashion, whether writing a blog post, posting on social media, or having a logo included somewhere with visibility.

THE BENEFITS OF A SPONSORSHIP

Clearly, the most obvious perk to a sponsorship is monetary, but there are more! Here are a few:

- Monetary or other support
- Establishing a connection with a brand
- Gaining credibility in a space
- Taking things to the next level

Monetary or Other Support

If you secure a sponsorship, it doesn't just have to be for money. As with trading service, there might be something else the brand could offer you in exchange. Maybe you need a cover design for your book, so you work with the design company on a package that gives them promotional credit on social media and your email list.

Establishing a Connection with a Brand

Working through a company like Social Fabric means you won't actually have direct contact with the brand itself. So you might be writing a post for Target, but you won't have any contact with Target. If you can work directly with a brand, you might be able to leverage that connection further in the future. Make sure you do the very best job you can fulfilling your part of the sponsorship!

Gaining Credibility in a Space

When you are hosting an event and have recognizable brands as your sponsors, it gives YOU credibility. Those brands believed enough in you to support you. I can tell you that when I invited people to my book launch, they sounded excited. But when I said it was sponsored by Kroger and the local Grateful Dane Distillery, there was a different LEVEL of excitement. This suddenly seemed like a legit party.

Taking Things to the Next Level

A sponsorship may not simply cover some costs for you. Securing a sponsorship might help you take things to the next level, one that wouldn't have been possible without the help and support. It could be the difference between reaching and exceeding your goals an expectations.

TIPS FOR GAINING SPONSORSHIPS

Chapter Five covers the perfect pitch, so knowing that information, I felt great about reaching out to sponsors. Until I tried to secure them for my book launch party. I had some traction, then stalled out. I had to call in the big guns, namely Bobbie Byrd of Blog Elevated who gave me a pep talk and some great tips. Here are some tips if you want to secure a sponsorship:

- Start with people you know
- Be clear on expectations and what you will offer
- Send out way more than you need
- Create a spreadsheet

Start with People You Know

My shortlist of sponsors almost all came through for me. That included ConvertKit and Mediavine in particular, two companies I use and love. ConvertKit is my email service provider and I run ads from Mediavine on my lifestyle blog. I already had contacts there (so an actual email that I know goes to an actual person) and they knew me. If you already have a relationship with a brand or have done a sponsored post before, start there!

Be Clear on Expectations and What You Will Offer

I've already talked about this in Chapter Five on pitches, but when you're asking for sponsorship, you need to be sure that all the big points are laid out. What exactly do you want them to provide? What will you provide in return? Be specific with your social media followers (if social sharing is a part of it) and exactly how many shares, blog posts, or more where you will link to them. Will you use images? Just text? Their logo? A particular hashtag? Don't be overwhelming in the first email, but do give them enough information that they can make a decision.

Send Out Way More Than You Need

Bobbie really helped me with this one. I was reaching out to a small handful, waiting until I heard back, then reaching out to more. Her advice was to stop that and instead reach out to way more sponsors than I thought I would need. If I reached out to two competing companies, that was fine as long as I didn't end up having both as sponsors. *(This might work for a larger-scale event, but for something smaller, not so much!)* Apparently you'll get a lot of rejections, so you should be prepped with lots of potential sponsors.

Keep a Spreadsheet

I got this tip from Jason Zook and his course, Get a Sponsor for Anything. (*Great name, right?)* It can get tricky quickly if you send out a lot of emails, so set up a spreadsheet that lets you track this well. This can include follow ups as well so you can remember if you sent that second email.

Finding sponsors for this book's launch party was quite a feat while also writing the book, but I could see doing this again for other creative endeavors. A sponsorship doesn't have to simply look like a blog post with disclosure at the top. *(Remember; always disclose!)* Think outside the box and find something that would be beneficial to you both.

26

CO-WRITING A BOOK

Commitment Level: Medium to High
Time Level: Medium to High

Writing a book alone can seem like a daunting task. So…would writing a book with someone else be easier or harder? The answer isn't so clear: It depends.

I've already mentioned that I dropped out of the education department at my school because of all the group work. Even if I'm not the one who ends up doing the work for everyone (*which has been the case about 90% of my life in groups*), I don't always work well with a team. I like speed and other people slow me down.

When it comes to the commitment and time, writing a book with another author can seem pretty heavy. On the flip side, the benefits can be pretty amazing. Let's dig into those!

THE BENEFITS OF CO-WRITING A BOOK

Here are a few easy-to-see benefits from writing a book with another author:

- Cross-promotion and platform sharing
- Authority and expertise
- Shared workload
- Learning new strategies and tips

Cross-Promotion and Platform Sharing

Even though promotion is basically the last thing that happens when it comes to a book launch, it's often what writers dread the most. Co-writing doesn't mean you'll have HALF the promotion, but it does mean that you'll shoulder the load with someone else. Your book will also have double the existing audience as potential customers.

Authority and Expertise

Seeing two names on the cover of a book does a few things. People will give both authors credit for being as much of an expert as the most well-known of the two. Which is to say that if you are partnering with someone who has a great reputation, that reputation now extends to you as well.

I think that it also gives a sense of authority to the book as a whole. Not just one person believes in this, but TWO. It must be good! Co-writing has that effect of giving extra credence and expertise to the authors.

Shared Workload

Do I need to explain this one? It can be a benefit and a challenge, though, depending on how well you work with other people or if you tend to work faster alone. You have to find the right balance and the right method of splitting up the writing, communicating, making sure the content is unified, and all of the things that will make a book by two authors work well.

The same exact workflow probably won't work with two different authors either. So while you will pick up some hacks for how to make this work after the first partnership, you'll have to evaluate this each time. Still—writing with another author means that you will share the word count, so as long as you can find your workflow with each other, this is a great benefit.

Learning New Strategies and Tips

As you find that perfect workflow for each partnership, you'll pickup new strategies along the way. You will learn about new tools and practices, some of which work for you and some of which will not. But as you start to dig into the process of writing and promoting and publishing with someone else, you will pick up many helpful skills, tools, and strategies from working so closely with your partner.

TIPS FOR CO-WRITING A BOOK FROM HONORÉE CORDER

All of the benefits of co-writing really hinge on who you work with, so because of the commitment level, definitely be smart about who you partner up with. I enlisted author extraordinaire Honorée Corder, who has published a great number of books, both alone and with other authors. Here's her take:

> I've been lucky--I've had more than a dozen co-authors and to a person, every single experience has been positive and enlightening at the same time.
>
> I suggest keeping in mind these three things when attempting to collaborate and co-write:
>
> 1. The relationship must be equal. When approaching another writing, working with someone who has the same goals, level of experience, and even platform size is helpful. Two equal parties coming together creates synergy and magic!
> 2. Good fences make good neighbors. Your intention is to have an incredible experience, create a solid product, and make some bank. Be sure to have a legal document, drafted by an attorney, signed by both parties, that spells out who is going to do what, and when. Include your financial arrangement as well.

3. Be easy to work with! Keep the lines of communication open, be flexible, and have fun!

I hope your collaborations are as delightful as mine have been!

If you want to connect further with Honorée, you can find her site here: http://honoreecorder.com/

Co-writing a book is definitely a deeper partnership that will take more time. It has many benefits to you personally and can open doors for more collaborations with other authors. It might even lead to marriage. *(Just read the next chapter…)*

27

WHEN COLLABORATIONS CHANGE YOUR LIFE

Writing a book together might be just the beginning of a longer, more intense collaboration. I'm going to let Roland Denzel from Eat Move Live 52 share his story and then I'll share some takeaways and tips.

COLLABORATIONS OUTSIDE OF BUSINESS WITH ROLAND DENZEL

My wife Galina and I have the ultimate collaboration when it comes to our health and fitness writing and business. We met and decided to write a men's fitness book together purely based on our different, but related backgrounds. She was a trainer and coach who'd worked with thousands, and I was a do-it-yourselfer who coached himself through losing over 100 pounds. As we wrote that first book, we learned who did what best and which of us loved and loathed certain tasks. We also fell in love, which complicated things, even though it was my secret plan all along.

As Galina and I expanded into projects beyond just writing books, we were sometimes surprised how our roles changed over time. Looking back, we shouldn't have been so surprised. If only we'd been more honest with ourselves back then. For instance, Galina is amazing in front of a camera. It's easy for her and she usually gets it right on the first take. I wanted to be amazing, too. I'm not, so I struggled and forced it, delaying projects that could have been done far faster if only I'd realized it sooner.

In a similar vein, I love editing our books, polishing the flow, and making our two very distinct writing styles work together, while still retaining our two voices. I also enjoy learning the tech side of our business, plus marketing, and writing to our mailing lists, clients, and students. She likes some of these things, too, but I love it.

Collaborators choose to work together because they want to be better than the sum of their parts. That can't happen until you honestly discover not only what you're good at, but bad at, and what you each enjoy.

Find out what each of you likes, loves, and hates to do. Be sure to review this every month or so. We all change over time. Finding out a year later that that you could have been far more productive with a simple shifting of duties is a shame and a lost opportunity.

There will always be tasks that each of you hate. Who hates it less? Who can do the hated task faster? Can it be more easily and effectively outsourced? A collaboration doesn't have to stop at two people, especially with the wealth of contractors, consultants, and artists available online these days.

Tasks are often more than the task itself. If performing a task ruins your ability to do work before or after, it has to be rethought. Some jobs take so much out of me that I'm effectively ruined for the rest of the day. On-camera video is my nemesis, leaving me frustrated, angry, and tired. Galina, on the other hand, can be on-camera for hours and move on to the next thing happy as a clam. She was happy to take over the majority of our on camera work, and the whole business has been more productive since!

Don't be precious. If your partner thinks something doesn't work, be open to change. In the writing world, it's being willing to "kill your darlings." Darlings aren't your favorite characters, although they can be. Darlings are projects, words, pictures, or ideas that you love, even when they don't fit. Snip them from that project, but never delete them fully. If you really love it you might find a home for your l'il darling down the road.

Keep an open mind. It's a business, and in order to succeed sometimes you have to listen to constructive criticism.

Conversely, always be kind, especially when being honest. You're collaborating because of the relationship as much as the business. Both have to be healthy in order to succeed.

Connect with Roland on his site: http://eatmovelive52.com/

COLLABORATION TAKEAWAYS

I love Roland's story. Not just because it has a happy ending, but because of the great things he shared about how this business + life collab works. Let's break down some of the important points he mentioned:

- Split tasks based on skills
- Be open to change
- Kill your darlings

Split Tasks Based on Skills

While I think collaborations are great places to learn new skills, if you are constantly trying to do things that aren't already in your wheelhouse, you'll slow down the works. Balance learning from each other and sticking with your strengths.

Be Open to Change

I totally related to Roland's story about insisting on video when it was hard for him and easy for Galina. I've totally been there. I think that when we are open to things going wrong or sideways (*because they will*) or just willing to try new things or listen to advice, these partnerships will work the best.

Kill Your Darlings

As a writer, I've been hearing this quote for years. Nothing will help you identify your darlings like working with another person. You might notice things naturally in contrast with the other person or if you have a wise *(and kind)* partner, they might graciously help you see those darlings. This goes along with being open, but it especially speaks to being open to changing something you might hold really close.

Roland and Galina have a unique story, but there are so many elements that are common to all collaborations. Whether yours bleed over into a personal relationship outside of business or not, being open to what you can learn from that other person is a great perk.

28

GO AND COLLABORATE!

You have some tips. You have some specific ideas of collaborations. I hope your wheels are turning and you feel energized to reach out to other people. Even if, like me, you have plenty of horror stories from group projects.

So…what next?

I want to help you bridge the gap between learning and doing. I mean, I love being a nerd, but if you just take in the info and don't do anything with it, you're missing a big piece.

You've got the tools. You've got the ideas.

Where do you find the people to collaborate with?

I originally outlined this chapter in the first part of the book, where I talk about the attitude and the pitches and the other practical bits. But as I feel like the best place to leave you as I close the book is to send you out, here are a few of my favorite places to make connections AND tips for making them just about anywhere.

THE BEST PLACES TO MAKE CONNECTIONS

I'm going to share my very favorite, most impactful, and maybe surprising places to make connections:

- Twitter
- Live Events

Yes, you can connect on LinkedIn and Facebook and *(maybe?)* Google Plus and Reddit and Quora and Medium and so many other places! If you have a place you love and are making connections, awesome. Don't give that up. But if you aren't sure where to start, these are my picks and I'll share exactly why.

Twitter

Surprised? I know I've already mentioned the connecting power of Twitter, but I still think this is the one platform that gets a bad rap because people are missing out on the purpose. Twitter isn't just a link dump. *(Though it's kind of become that.)* It isn't about auto-DMs. *(Please just don't!)*

Twitter is perhaps the quickest way to actually connect with people and brands, especially people and brands who have a much larger following or platform than you do. This is not true across the board, but I have a few examples to illustrate. *(You can also hear me talking about this in episode 112 of the Create If Writing podcast: http://createifwriting.libsyn.com/112-connections-that-lead-to-collaborations)*

In terms of responsiveness, Twitter is often the best direct line. Better than a real person and better than a phone number. At least, if you've had a bad experience. After having a terrible experience in a hotel a few years ago, I talked with the manager at the hotel and has zero response. I tried calling the corporate line and got one of those automated menus. Then I took to Twitter.

Within five minutes of tweeting and tagging the hotel company, I was on the phone with an actual person, getting our issue resolved.

I've seen that same quick response from many influencers and even celebrities. Sure, some have that hired out. But when it comes to bigger people in your niche, often this is a great way to make that first connection.

The very first tiny writers' group I started had its roots in Twitter. I literally just sent a tweet out into the void asking if a few women writers or bloggers wanted to be in a small group. I called it the Writer's Bra. For a few years we stayed in communication daily or weekly in a little Facebook group. We've all drifted with school and kids, but that group really helped my focus! And I got to hire a trusted editor from the group for this book. *(Thanks, Sarah!!)*

If you want to find people on Twitter and begin connecting, you can use hashtags or advanced Twitter search. (*Not the same as the normal search: https://twitter.com/search-advanced?lang=en*) Try Twitter chats for real-time interaction. When people DO use Twitter, it's for real. And while many other platforms boast bigger growth and shiny things, Twitter still has the big players AND the media.

Live Events

I can trace back many of my current connections to my very first blog conference, Blog Elevated. I was a volunteer and got to hang out in the "green room" with the speakers. I had almost never talked with other bloggers in person and had zero plans to leverage relationships or connections. I was simply excited to be there and hang out.

At Blog Elevated I met Kami Huyse, the founder of Houston Social Media Breakfast. Later I met other social media influencers at HSMB, including Madalyn Sklar and Cheval John and Rebecca Councill and Kristyna Torres-Cruz. I had the privilege of speaking at Houston Social Media Breakfast twice

I also met Paula Rollo at Blog Elevated, a fellow blogger who collaborated with me to run the Profitable Blogging Summit for two years. Somehow passing each other in the hall at the first conference saying, "hi," turned into paid collaborations and a lot of support when we each when through hard struggles.

At BlogHer Food I got to share the stage with Laura Fuentes of Momables, after hearing her speak at Blog Elevated a few years before. I met Jillian Tohber-Leslie, the founder of the MiloTree App. I got to be the first interview as she launched her podcast and she has become a huge source of encouragement and support.

A representative from Mediavine heard me speak at BlogHer Food and asked me to speak at the Mediavine Publishers Conference the next year. Now Mediavine is also sponsoring my book launch.

I could go on, but you see the point: My most powerful collaborations started at in-person events.

While digital events are amazing and easy, there is something about a live connection that makes a fast impact and allows you to really network in a different way. For me, the best connections came not from me wandering around looking for them. I just talked with people around me, carried on normal conversations, and often followed up with people that I connected with.

To circle back to Blog Elevated, I still talk with founders Lisa Stauber and Bobbie Byrd on the regular and turned to Bobbie when I needed help putting together sponsorship packages. They are huge and generous resources to their speakers, the attendee community at large, and the local community. If you are looking for a live event, try to find one where you see those qualities in the people heading it up! *(And find out more from Blog Elevated- http://blogelevated.com!)*

You simply can't know what will come from meeting someone in person! Thinking back to mindset, it's so important to go into an event wanting to connect, but not necessarily placing weight expectations on a relationship. Many of the amazing partnerships were months or years in the making.

I didn't walk into any of those live events thinking I was going to carry so much away from them. I simply showed up, handed out business cards, and had actual conversations. The impact has blown me away.

TIPS FOR CONNECTING

I don't have a bullet point list and a lot of explanation for how to connect well, as I've already covered a lot of this, and my best advice boils down to being HUMAN and treating other people like HUMANS.

Talk to people and treat people like people.

Listen.

Ask questions.

Be interested in what they do and helpful if that makes sense in the situation.

Don't monopolize the conversation with your awesomeness.

Don't silently try to figure out how this person will help you get ahead.

I'm not saying you can't think about opportunities or be excited to meet someone or that you shouldn't talk to someone if you do secretly hope that they'll read your blog and ask you to be on their podcast. We all have those secret hopes and I know that sometimes I meet someone important and forget to be human and just totally fangirl.

But as much as you can, don't have a single-mindedness about networking. It shows. It's a turnoff. Maybe it will work with some, but it isn't a good practice and will catch up with you sometime.

Follow up with people, whether after an event or when you have a conversation on Twitter or in a Facebook group. See how you interact. Let things unfold. Be open to organic partnerships and opportunities. Give back when you can.

As I've said again and again, these partnerships and collaborations have done more for me than any tool or app or scheduler or five-step formula. Relying on people can be messier and harder, but have much more far-reaching effects.

Go forth and collaborate!

(And don't forget to get in on the bonus materials! I'd also love to hear from you if you make amazing connections or have questions. There is a free Facebook group JUST for people who access the bonus material. So head over there if you haven't already: http://createifwriting.com/collabbonus)

ACKNOWLEDGEMENTS

It would NOT be a book about collaborations if I didn't have a very HUGE list of people to thank.

I'll start with the brands that help sponsor the launch for Creative Collaborations:

- ConvertKit
- MediaVine
- Grateful Dane Distillery
- Kroger

I'd also love to thank my editor, Sarah Steidl. Especially for handling things when I send them to you and say I need them TOMORROW OR ELSE MY BOOK WILL NEVER LAUNCH.

Thanks also to my book cover designer, James from Go On Write. I highly recommend his covers if you need one! http://www.goonwrite.com

A massive thank you to the Create If Writing Community, both the lovely and wild free group and those supporters who joined the paid community and have stuck around for over a year (!!!). You guys are seriously the best.

Thank you to Team Kiki, my launch team who was so passionate about supporting me and this book!

A few people did not contribute to the book, but are just as much a part of it for the LIFE SUPPORT. Big thanks to:

- Taylor Bradford (http://bossgirlcreative.com) for all the support, late night chats, and inspiration.

- Jillian Tohber-Leslie (http://catchmyparty.com) for writing down some powerful words in my journal. I won't forget them.

- Lisa Stauber & Bobbie Byrd for fostering awesome community here in Houston and helping me see the power in local roots. (http://blogelevated.com)

- Mom & Dad & Geoff. You know what you did. (Basically PUT UP WITH ME FOR YEARS.)

And to all of the lovely contributors who graced the pages of this book, THANK YOU. This book would not have portrayed the power of collaboration with all of you. I am so thankful for all that I've learned from each of you! In order you appeared in the book, thank you:

Kami Huyse – http://www.zoeticamedia.com/
Danielle Liss – http://businessese.com
Jane Friedman – http://janefriedman.com
Bailey Richert – http://baileyrichert.com
Nicole Culver – http://nicoleculver.co
Bryan Cohen – http://bryancohen.com
Meera Kothand – http://meerakothand.com
Mandi Ehman – http://www.lifeyourway.com
Marianne West – http://sustainablelivingpodcast.com
Amy Schmittauer – http://vloglikeaboss.com
Summer Tannhauser – http://summertannhauser.com
Chris Syme – http://cksyme.com
Jamie Davis – http://jamiedavisbooks.com
Madalyn Sklar – http://madalynsklar.com
Paula Rollo – http://beautythroughimperfection.com

Andi Cumbo-Floyd – http://andilit.com
Honorée Corder – http://honoreecorder.com
Roland Denzel – http://eatmovelive52.com

I'm so glad that I know people like you guys and can call you friends, colleagues, and besties. THANK YOU!

ABOUT THE AUTHOR

Kirsten Oliphant has an MFA in Fiction from the University of North Carolina at Greensboro but spends most of her time wrangling her five kids and building a digital empire.

She is the host of the Create If Writing podcast, the author of *Email Lists Made Easy for Writers and Bloggers* and *31 Small Steps to Grow Your Blog*. She has spoken at events like Podcast Movement, Blog Elevated, MediaVine Publishers Conference, Houston Social Media Breakfast, Social Media Day Houston, Houston Baptist Writer's Conference, the Business Advancement Conference, and more. In 2016 and 2017 she was named one of Houston's Top 25 Social Media Power Influencers.

You can find her hanging out at: http://createifwriting.com

Join the community of Create Ifs: http://createifwriting.com/community

Want a weekly email with news, resources, and links related to writing, blogging, and social media? Register here: http://createifwriting.com/quickfix

MORE GREAT READS FROM KIRSTEN OLIPHANT

Get a Free Guide to Help Plan Your Year

Learn to plan strategically for a full year of content. Blog posts, books, social media, and more. Find it here: http://a.co/96QJctk

Email Lists Made Easy for Writers and Bloggers

Learn to apply all those amazing marketing techniques when you don't feel like a marketer. This book breaks down why you need an email list, how to set it up, and the important aspects of using your list to turn your readers into raving fans.

Get your copy today! http://a.co/155Bgbc

31 Small Steps to Grow Your Blog

This book breaks down blog growth into manageable (often repeatable) steps. You'll also learn the kinds of revenue streams for your blog and why your blog isn't growing.

Order yours today! http://a.co/c0mxHMN

Made in the USA
Middletown, DE
18 March 2021